CW00503846

Taxes for Small Business & Credit Repair Secrets for Busy Entrepreneurs

2 Books in 1: The Beginner - Friendly Practical Guide to Understanding Taxes for Your Business & Unlock The Secrets Strategies Used by Credit Attorneys to Fix Your Bad Debt and Finally Change Your Financial Life

[LUCAS ANDERSON]

Taxes for Small Business

The First Guide in The Usa to Understanding Taxes for Your LLC and Sole Proprietorship Business Even If You've Never Submitted Tax Return Before and The 3 Secrets Tips to Reduce Taxes Legally

[LUCAS ANDERSON]

Legal & Disclaimer

The information contained in this book and its contents is not designed to replace or take the place of any form of medical or professional advice; and is not meant to replace the need for independent medical, financial, legal or other professional advice or services, as may be required. The content and information in this book has been provided for educational and entertainment purposes only.

The content and information contained in this book has been compiled from sources deemed reliable, and it is accurate to the best of the Author's knowledge, information and belief. However, the Author cannot guarantee its accuracy and validity and cannot be held liable for any errors and/or omissions. Further, changes are periodically made to this book as and when needed. Where appropriate and/or necessary, you must consult a professional (including but not limited to your doctor, attorney, financial advisor or such other professional advisor) before using any of the suggested remedies, techniques, or information in this book.

Upon using the contents and information contained in this book, you agree to hold harmless the Author from and against any damages, costs, and expenses, including any legal fees potentially resulting from the application of any of the information provided by this book. This disclaimer applies to any loss, damages or injury caused by the use and application, whether directly or indirectly, of any advice or information presented, whether for breach of contract, tort, negligence, personal injury, criminal intent, or under any other cause of action. You agree to accept all risks of using the information presented inside this book.

You agree that by continuing to read this book, where appropriate and/or necessary, you shall consult a professional (including but not limited to your doctor, attorney, or financial advisor or such other advisor as needed) before using any of the suggested remedies, techniques, or information in this book.

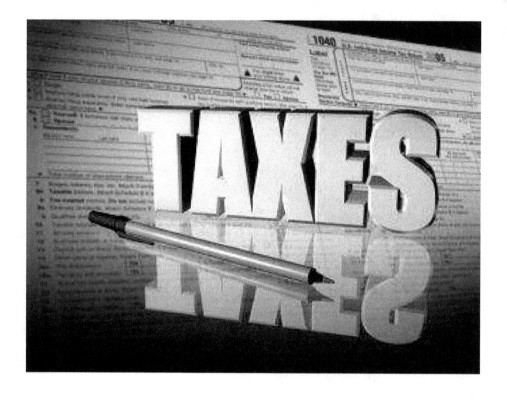

Table of Contents

Introduction

Welcome! First of all, thank you and congratulations for downloading this book. I really appreciate you putting your time and trust in me. I am truly convinced that this book is able to provide you with the value and information you are looking for.

If every year you have someone else doing your taxes without really understanding how you can minimize the amount of tax you pay and what influences the amount of income tax you pay, then chances are that you're missing out on a lot of additional money year after year. Taxes don't have to be complicated to understand. As long as you have a grasp on the basics then you can figure out ways to minimize the amount of money that you pay in taxes while maximizing the amount of money that stays in your bank account.

By the time you are finished reading this book, you'll understand how taxes are paid, what you can do to reduce the amount of taxes you pay, and have a basic understanding of taxes in general. With the techniques that you learn here you'll save money and time, by making your tax return audit proof and making sure that you aren't missing out on opportunities to significantly and legally reduce the amount you pay in taxes.

The tax laws in this country benefit small business and home-based business owners. You can enjoy doing what you love on the side and make a business from your passions while getting significant tax reductions and other benefits. The money that you spend on transportation, food, and lodging can reduce your taxes throughout the year and minimize the amount you pay each year.

Section I provides you with an overview of tax basics by going over how taxes started in the United States, how taxes are calculated, and how to uncover tax breaks that will save you money. Section II covers specific ways that you can reduce your taxes year after year by forming a business, teaches you about deductions, and explains the different ways to shelter your money.

11

Chapter 1: Tax Basics

Small businesses, even if not formed as corporations, are required to calculate the total profits earned or losses incurred by their business operations for income tax purposes. This tax information is then included in the business owners' personal income tax returns so there is no need for them to prepare a separate tax return for their business.

Since the tax returns of a business are filed with personal tax returns of the owners, their deadlines normally coincide with the deadline of personal tax returns. If the deadline occurs on a holiday or a weekend, the deadline is then automatically moved to the following business day.

A small business that is not formed as a corporation is normally one of the following business types, although there might be slight variations in the different states in the US:

- **Sole Proprietorship:** This is the default type of your business if you did not specify any business type upon registration of your business. A sole proprietorship company is required to pay its income taxes through the personal income tax return of the owner or a sole proprietor. You will have to prepare Schedule C (Profit or Loss for a Small Business) for the computation of the business' profit or loss that is then combined with the other income of the owner and filed in Form 1040.

- **Partnership:** As the name implies, a partnership is composed of two or more partners and their business is normally registered with a particular state. Partnerships are required to file their information tax returns through Form 1065. Each partner receives a copy of their Schedule K-1 that reflects their share or portion of the profits earned or losses incurred by the partnership. Each partner will then include the income or loss reflected on their Schedule K-1's on their personal income tax return (Form 1040).

- **Limited Liability Company (LLC):** This particular business type is not liable for any federal income tax. An LLC, that has one owner (single-member LLC), pays its income tax similar to a sole proprietorship. An LLC, that has several members (multiple-member LLC), pays its income tax similar to a partnership.

It is not enough for you to fill up the various income tax returns or forms when paying your taxes. You also need to submit other documents including audited financial statements that will support the data reflected on your income tax returns. These supporting documents will include the following and other pertinent documents:

- **Comparative balance sheet** for the end of the current fiscal year and the prior year
- **Comparative profit and loss statement** (or commonly known as income state) for both the current and prior fiscal years
- **Supporting schedule** that reflects the calculation of cost of goods sold

Here is other tax information you need to be aware of:

• A person who manages his own business is required to pay **self-employment taxes** (Social Security tax and Medicare tax) for him or herself at the rate of 15.3 percent on his earnings.

• **You have two options in filing your tax returns**. You can either submit it through mail or you can access the Electronic Filing and Tax Payment System (EFTPS) of the Internal Revenue Service (IRS).

• **If, for some reason, you cannot file your income tax return on the prescribed due,** you have the option to apply for an automatic extension for filing both your small business and personal taxes. The extension that will be granted to you will usually be for 6 months. This means that you will have until October 15 of the same the year to file your income tax returns. But you need to be aware that the extension that will be granted to you will not include an extension for any tax payments that you need to make. Even with an approved deadline extension, you will still have to remit any estimated taxes on or before April 15. A sole proprietor or a single-member LLC can apply for an extension for their personal tax return using Form 4868. A partnership or a multiple-member LLC, on the other hand, can use Form 7004.

• **There are instances when the financial information reflected on the tax returns have been filed as erroneous.** The errors may either be on the computation of the business taxes or the personal taxes of the business owner. In such cases, you are required to submit an amended tax return that will reflect the correct financial information. The forms that you can use to submit your amended tax return depend on the business.

o **For personal returns**, you can file your amended tax return using Form 1040X-Amended Return.

o **For partnerships**, you can still use Form 1065 but you need to tick box G (5) found on page 1. You are also required to attach a separate statement that specifies the line number(s) of the items that you revised, the amended amount, the revised treatment that you used in computation and justifications for the revisions made.

o   If you submitted a partnership tax return and later found errors on your Schedule K-1 or if the revisions to Form 1065 will result to changes in the information of your Schedule K-1, you need to file an amended Schedule K-1. You need to tick the "Amended K-1" box found on the top of the form to indicate denote that the form has been revised. You then need to give a copy of the revised Schedule K-1 to the appropriate partner or member so they can revise their own Form 1040.

- **All throughout the year, withholding or retention taxes would have been withheld from your wages or incomes.** Those withheld taxes are the government's control in making that businesses will not evade their tax responsibilities.   But normally, the taxes withheld from you may not be sufficient to cover total taxes you need to pay for the whole year. In such cases, you are required to pay estimated taxes for the remaining unpaid balance.

Nobody would forget the sinking feeling you would have experienced, whether it was your high school job at the local café or your first job after college, when you would have eagerly opened your paycheck, already planning a list of things you need, only to realize that a substantial chunk of your salary is missing!

If you haven't experienced this yet, then be prepared because it is a really bad feeling. Yes, you guessed it right, that missing chunk out of your paycheck went to taxes. Don't be under the misconception that you aren't getting anything in return for it. Some of the examples of what the taxes you paid get you are the clean drinking water from your tap, police who ensure that your neighborhood is safe and also the garbage that gets picked up from your curbside.

In this chapter I will explain the ins and outs of taxes so that you can fully understand the manner in which they can affect your finances.

Brief overview of taxes

To put it simply, taxes are the compulsory contributions that you are required to make to the state you reside in, and also to the federal government, that is levied by the government to pay for all the things that are required for the society as a whole. This includes everything from providing law enforcement, the salaries of the armed forces, the roads that you drive on to the salary of the President as well. Payment of taxes is not optional and there really is no way that you can outrun paying your dues. In a survey it was found out that about 96% of Americans considered it to be their basic civic duty to pay their taxes. So, the best thing that you can do is to obtain a basic understanding of taxes in order to be able to pay them on time and also pay the accurate amount, without much stress- both financial as well as emotional.

Why is it important to understand taxes

Having a good understanding of taxes will help you save when you are filing them. It is noticed that about $945 million is overpaid to the government by the American citizens on a yearly basis. That comes up to about $400 per household; this is an unnecessary expenditure that can be avoided altogether if you are a little careful and can understand about the system of taxation. Not just this, but understanding about taxes will also help save you at work. By understanding the system of taxation you can manage to save a couple of hundreds of dollars on transportation costs incurred or even childcare and so on. The other advantage of understanding about taxes is that it will help you get a better idea of your budget. You will be able to carry on with your monthly planning in a better fashion and the yearly spending as well, if you can understand how much you are supposed to be paying. Frankly, no one really likes financial surprises unless it happens to be a windfall gain.

Working   of   taxes

Whenever you pay taxes, this money directly goes into the coffers of the government whether local, state or federal. This money is pooled together and then allocated to different projects and services, ranging anywhere from the regulatory agencies that are entrusted with the work of ensuring that the medicines you consume are safe and that the roads you drive on aren't filled with potholes. The tax system is really complicated, but then again there are a lot of regulations set in place that will help you increase your savings and will also help you send more wisely. For instance, if you take any money out of the 401(k) for anything other than your retirement then it isn't good; the government can levy an additional tax penalty along with the ordinary taxes that you are supposed to pay, in the form of punishment. The other instance would be when you decide to donate to any charity, and then the government will reward you for this by reducing your tax liability.

Terms you need to know

Withholding: This is the amount that is taken out of every paycheck you receive in order to pay for the income tax at the end of the year. When you fill out the W-4 form at your job, you will be able to designate what your withholding will exactly be.

Deduction: This is similar to a discount on tax, this happens to be a dollar amount that can be subtracted from your income that is taxable and thereby reduces the amount on which you are liable to pay tax for.

IRS: IRS stands for Internal Revenue Service and this is a government agency that is solely responsible for the collection of taxes from all those who are liable to pay taxes according to the law.

Capital gains: This is the profit that you would receive from investments on capital assets like stock, bond or even real estate. Capital gain is the difference between the selling price and the purchase price.

For instance, you have purchased stock for $10 and you have sold it for $20, your capital gain on such a transaction would be $10.

The common types of taxes you need to know about:

There are different types of taxes, but following are the ones that you need to know about.

Payroll tax

Everything that is taken out of the paycheck you receive is the payroll tax. This includes the federal as well as the state income taxes, Medicare tax and social security tax withholding as well, it also includes a couple of local taxes that includes city, county or school district taxes and also the state disability or unemployment insurance.

Sales tax:

This is the tax that is levied by the state government and you might not have realized this yet, but you end up paying this tax whenever you buy something. If you reside in Delaware, Oregon, Alaska, Montana or New Hampshire, there is no sales tax here. The rate of sales tax varies from one state to another. For instance, it is about 8.75% in California and 4% in Hawaii. Sales tax is always included in the receipt you are given whenever you make a purchase or avail a service. The next time you go to a restaurant, you can notice this in the receipt that they give you. Once you have paid this tax, you needn't worry about paying it again for the same transaction. The tax that is charged on every sale is sales tax.

Income tax:

Income tax like the name suggests is the tax that you are bound to pay at the end of year to the federal and the state governments. If you are engaged in a salaried employment, then this amount is withheld from your monthly paychecks. At the end of the year, you need to calculate how much you owe and accordingly if you have paid excess then the government shall refund the rest, but if you have paid too little, then you will need to pay the rest. If you happen to be a freelancer, then you are supposed to pay the quarterly taxes. If not, then it is your responsibility to pay what you owe to the government in full in the month of April and this can include the penalty for the nonpayment of tax. For instance, if you are earning $1000 a year as a freelancer, then you are supposed to save up at least 30% of this for the purpose of taxes and I would advise you to talk to your tax advisor as soon as you can to ensure that you are indeed setting aside the correct amount.

Property tax:

This is the tax that is levied by the government on your home and all the property that you own; it could be a piece of land or your cabin in the woods. You will be taxed on all the property you own regardless of it being free or clear of nay charges of mortgage. As long as the property is registered in your name, you are liable to pay this tax. The local government usually collects this tax and it goes towards the funding of local schools, law enforcement, development and maintenance of roads and more such functions. You might pay this tax on a semi-annual basis and it often a part of your monthly mortgage payments so that you don't have to pay a lump sum amount in April.

Capital gains tax:

Capital gain is the profit that you make on the sale of your investment. The difference between the low cost price and the comparatively higher selling price gives you the capital gain. For instance, you purchased stock for $100 and have sold it for $120, the capital gain you have incurred is $20 and the government will levy a tax on the $20 you have made. In case you have sold this investment before the end of the year, that is you haven't held it for a year, and then you needn't pay capital gains tax, you will just need to pay the normal income tax that includes short term capital gains as well. In a bid to encourage long-term investments, if you manage to hold onto the investments for a year or any longer then you are entitled for a capital gains tax that is lower. You will need to pay this tax along with all the other taxes in the month of April.

Chapter 2: What Is Tax Code

Value Added Tax

The Value Added Tax is a form of sales tax that is subject to the purchase of most goods and services. It must be collected and submitted by the retailers or sellers to the government revenue department of the United States. The standard rate of Value Added Tax in the US is determined by the central planning authority and by the state itself. Currently, the tax rate in the United States is 10 percent. However, the standard rate of VAT is set to 15 percent. Other than these rates, many local rates are imposed by the state after the reduction. This is based on the availability and the size of service sector operations in that state. Such reduced taxes are called a truncated rate and range from 1.5 percent to 10 percent.

If your business is located in the USA you don't have to pay VAT tax.

Income Tax

In the United States, the rate that is levied in the form of income tax varies from organizational structure to structure. The tax rate imposed on the sole traders and pass-through entities are basically similar to the rate the individuals and owners are liable to pay on their incomes. For the last year 2019, the personal income tax rates depended on the income level and filing status. It ranges from 10 percent to 37 percent.

Sales Tax

The rates of General Sales Tax, commonly referred to as GST, might be different in various states and localities in the USA. Despite that, no law in the US can implement the federal sales tax. Still, different localities in 45 US states impose sales tax on producers and consumers. In these states, the business owners and management are assigned the responsibility to calculate, collect, and report the sales tax to local and state governments.

For customers, the amount of sales tax is already included in the price of the product they purchase. The sales tax is to be paid during the purchase of goods and services when they pay for the utility. Recently, in a session, the court decided that even some e-commerce sellers and retailers should initiate the collection and reporting of sales tax from the customers, purchasing from outside the state. Being the owner of a small business, it is essential to know about the rules and regulations subject to the sales tax levied in your state and locality.

Social Security Tax

For the year 2019, the rate of Social Security Tax had been set to 12.4 percent. It is imposed on the wages paid above the $128,400. Usually, it is the responsibility of an employer to pay ½ of this percentage, which means 6.2%. In contrast, the remaining half of the Social Security tax is taken out from the employee's paycheck. But if you are a self-employed individual, the self-employment taxes are to be paid by you in full.

Self-Employment Tax

Self-employment taxes are imposed on self-employed individuals, which includes Social Security and Medicare. Individuals are responsible for paying such taxes only if their net earnings from self-employment last year are either $400 or more. Almost all businesses pick up half of the responsibility for contributing to the Social Security and Medicare taxes on their employee's wages. In contrast, the other half of the tax is collected or deducted with consent from the employee's paycheck and remitted by the business. But in the case of self-employed individuals, they have to pay the entire amount for such taxes. However, for those self-employed individuals who are, for example, working for a church or on a fishing crew, special rules apply.

In the United States, the rate for self-employment tax is 15.3 percent. The rate is further divided into separate contributions, Social Security and Medicare. Social Security, which is the amount to be saved for employees to help them with their old-age, survivors, and disability insurance coverage consists of 12.4 percent. In contrast, the other part, Medicare or hospital insurance, consists of the leftover 2.9 percent of the tax.

Employment or Payroll Tax

The rate of employment or payroll taxes includes the following:

Federal Unemployment Tax

Currently, approximately 6% of the total Federal Unemployment Tax is imposed and deducted on the first $7,000 you pay to an employee. If you have paid state unemployment taxes, then you are eligible to claim it for a tax credit.

Medicare Tax

This type of tax is also split between the employer and the employee contribution. Without considering any threshold, 2.9 percent of the total wages is the rate that has to be paid for the Medicare tax. Individuals that are earning more than $200,000 each year are withheld with additional Medicare requirements.

Excise Tax

The rate of excise tax greatly depends on the different range of products you are selling on the market. Some states, in the US, charge this type of tax. The excise tax rate applicable today was first introduced in 2016, in which the top 1% earners were bound to face an average excise tax of 0.2%, whereas the bottom 20 percent of earners are subjected to a rate of 1.8 percent.

State Unemployment Tax

In the United States, each state is given the right to decide the rate of unemployment tax to be charged. While determining the rate of unemployment tax, generally the years of operation and size of the enterprise, the industry it is categorized under, the typical turnover rate, and the number of former employees who have filed for unemployment benefits are taken into consideration.

Property Tax

When considering the nature of sales tax when determining its rate imposed, property tax is almost the same. Property tax also varies massively based on the country, state, and town, where your owned property exists. Each time an individual or a business purchases a property, whether an office or a multi-story bungalow, registering it with the local tax authorities is one of the priorities. The agency will then send you the information regarding the tax rates imposed on your property and the deadlines before which you will have to file the taxes. Property taxes are imposed on the assessed value of the property and not the price you purchased it for or the current market value.

Import Duties

The rate of tax applicable for import duties varies from country to country, depending on the aim and objectives of the government. Import duty is considered to be a protectionist policy that a country implements to reduce imports and improve the balance of payments. It is one of the legal barriers a country might keen to use to restrict imports.

In the US, approximately 96 percent of imported merchandise is industrial goods. It means that each year, the US government has to maintain its foreign currency reserves and also has to increase exports. These cancel out the negative effect created through the burden of imports.

Chapter 3: How Government Collects Taxes: Federal, State, County and City Level

There are many types of taxes that can be levied and you have to know them in order to successfully pay them. In this chapter, we will look at the main taxes that are levied on a business.

Federal taxes

The first and most important tax that you should know about is the federal tax. Federal taxes are imposed on small businesses, depending on how much profit they make. This tax will be different from what you will pay to your state. Federal taxes are possibly the biggest sum that you will pay, as the margin levied is quite large. In case of businesses that have employees, you have to submit employees' tax holdings along with payroll taxes and social security taxes. In order to pay your federal taxes, you will have to make use of the right forms, which are as follows.

Sole Proprietor: Form 1040 Schedule C or C-EZ and additionally Schedule F for a farm business.

Partnership: Form 1065 in order to submit profits and gains. Remember that a partnership firm only disburses its profits to partners.

C Corporations: Form 1120

S Corporations: Form 1120S

Limited Liability Company: Form 1040 with Schedules C, E and F.

You have to submit your forms 1020, 1020S and 1120A to the IRS by 15th March every year, for the previous year.

Form 1040, 1065 and Schedule C should be submitted to the IRS by April 15th.

It is extremely important for you to pay your federal taxes in case you want to avoid any problems.

State level taxes

State level taxes refer to the taxes that your particular state will levy on your business. Each and every individual state in the US has its very own laws, which means that you have to know your state's laws in detail in order to file for taxes.

The rules can vary for sole proprietor, LLC and startup firms. Based on the business that you are carrying out, you have to go through the different tax laws that your company might be subject to.

Apart from collecting company taxes, these states also collect sales taxes. Sales taxes are levied on the sale of products and services. If the company has bought goods for its operation from outside the state, then a tax will be levied on it as well. This type is better known as *use tax* and you have to pay it in order to avoid discrepancies.

However, if you as a company have bought goods for retail sale, then no taxes will be levied on it.

City taxes

City taxes are also levied on business by the city's government in order to operate legally. But this is always just a one-time expense for the business. In exchange, the company will get a legal permit and also government recognition, both of which are important for a company to fare well.

County taxes

County taxes are levied on those businesses that operate in a particular county. How much needs to be paid will depend on the rules set by the particular county. The tax is mostly levied on any vehicles, buildings or other physical goods that the company owns.

These form the different types of taxes that can be levied on your company by the IRS. You have to bear in mind that you will have to pay all of these and make room for them in your annual budget. If you have been filing taxes for some time now, then you will know to keep a substantial sum ready to direct towards taxes. But if this is your first year in paying taxes then you have to know to keep a particular sum aside to pay your taxes.

Chapter 4: Accounting Lingo

As a business owner, you have a long list of tasks to complete, and now that your business is off the ground, you should focus on the accounting tasks that will come along with owning a business. In this chapter, we will look at some steps that you must complete to help you cover your bases in accounting.

Open a Bank Account

Once you register the business, you need to find a place to stash the income. It is a good idea to maintain separate records since this will help you when you file taxes. A Corporation, partnership, and LLC must have a bank account that is different from the owner's bank account. A business that follows the sole proprietorship structure does not require a separate bank account, but it is recommended that the owner separate his personal account from the business account for better accounting and tax paperwork.

You should first open a business checking account and then create a savings account to organize the funds. You can also use these accounts to plan your taxes. For example, you can set up the savings account and save a small percentage of every payment as the self-employment tax that you withhold. You can also consider a business credit card. Most LLCs and Corporations have separate credit cards to avoid mingling business and personal assets.

You need to perform due diligence before you open an account in the bank. Do your research about different banks and the different types of accounts they offer and look at the fee structure for these accounts. Every bank charge a business checking account a higher rate when compared to a personal checking account, so calculate what you will owe the bank before you open an account there. If you want to open a business bank account, you can have a business name and also register this account in your province or state. You can check with individual banks to identify the documents you should bring to the appointment.

Track the Expenses

You must develop a solid business record keeping method to effectively track all your expenses. This is an important step since it will help you build financial statements, monitor the growth of your business, prepare tax returns, support your reports on your tax returns and keep track of any deductible expenses.

You need to establish this system when you start the business since it will help you organize any important records and receipts. This is a simple and old process, and you can use a FiloFax or a service such as ShoeBoxed. The IRS does not require you to maintain receipts for a transaction below $75, but it is best if you maintain them. You must pay attention to the following types of receipts:

Meals and Entertainment

When you conduct a business meeting in a restaurant or café, you should document it in your books. Record the names of the people who attended the meeting and the purpose of that meeting.

Business Travel

The CRA and IRS are wary of individuals who claim deductions on their personal activities as well as their business expenses. The receipts you save will provide a paper trail for the business activities.

Vehicle-Related Expenses

You should record when, why, and where you used a specific vehicle for your business. You should apply the percentage of use to the vehicle that you claim expenses for. Most states allow a 100% deduction on gas mileage costs, so make sure to track the records and keep a log of the business miles.

Gift Receipts

If you receive gifts from your customers or clients, it matters if the giver goes to the event with you. If the giver does, this type of expense is an entertainment expense and not a gift. Remember to note this information at the back of the receipt.

Home Office Receipts

This receipt is similar to the vehicle receipt. You must calculate the percentage of your house you use for the business, and apply this percentage to the expenses.

It is good to start your business at home if you want to reduce the overhead cost. You will also qualify for some tax breaks since you can deduct the portion of your house that you use for the business. You can also deduct the amount you spend on the Internet, transportation from work sites, business errands, and your cell phone.

If an expense is for both personal life and business, you must ensure that it reflects the mixed-use. For example, if you have one cell phone, you must deduct the amount you spend on business calls and messages.

Develop the Bookkeeping System

Bookkeeping is the process where you record the daily transactions and categorize them. At the end of every working day, you must reconcile the bank statements.

Accounting is a very high-level process, and it looks only at the progress that the business makes. It will look at the different transactions and compile the data from the bookkeeping software or material to build financial statements. As the business owner, you must determine the method you want to use for bookkeeping:

• You can choose to do it yourself and use different software and tools such as Wave or QuickBooks. You can also use a simple Excel spreadsheet to help you with the same.

• You can choose to outsource the process or hire a part-time bookkeeper.

- If you have a large business, you can hire employees to do your bookkeeping and maintain the accounts.

Since you have multiple options, you can choose the method that works best for you. American business owners must determine if they want to use the accrual method or the cash method for accounting. Let us look at the difference between these methods:

- **Cash Method:** In this method, the company will recognize the revenue and expense when they receive or pay the amount.
- **Accrual Method:** In this method, you should recognize the revenues and expenses when the transaction occurs, even if the transaction is not out or in the bank account. The business must, however, track the payables and receivables.

According to the new tax reform, small businesses in the United States can use the cash method instead of the accrual method.

Set up the Payroll System

As a new business owner, you may choose to run a one-person show. You may choose to hire someone to help you later or maybe hire a freelancer to help you design the logo or market your business. Before you do this, you should establish whether the individual you hire is an independent contractor or employee. If the individual is an employee, you should set up a payroll schedule and ensure that you levy the correct taxes before you transfer money into their account. If the individual is an independent contractor, you must track the amount you pay for each person. You must file a form for each contractor at the end of the fiscal year.

Understand Import Tax

If you plan to import or purchase goods from other countries, you must understand the rate the Federal and state government will charge you. The amount charged will vary depending on the business structure. When you import products, you are subject to import taxes and duties, and you must understand these charges better if you run a dropshipping firm. Your country will impose these fees when you import goods. You should learn about the rates that the US charges you when you import goods and also any associated taxes. This will help you determine the rules from the beginning. You can also use an online calculator to help you estimate the fee and also plan for any additional costs.

Determine Your Pay

When the sales roll in, you need to find a way to accept the payments. If you run your business on Shopify, you can use the payments application or widget on Shopify to accept any credit card payments. This will save you the trouble of setting up a third party payment gateway or merchant account. If you want to accept the payments without using the Shopify widget or application, you need to set up a third party payment processor such as PayPal or a merchant account.

The latter is a bank account that will allow your business to accept any payment directly from the customer. If you choose to use a third-party payment processor, the gateway will charge you anywhere between 2.9% of the amount per transaction. Make sure to perform due diligence before you choose a third party payment gateway.

Establish the Procedures to Calculate Sales Tax

If you run an eCommerce business, you know that the sales tax regulations are different for every state. Each state will levy a different tax rate depending on the location of the business. The same goes for a small business or startup. If a customer walks into a retail store, they will pay a sales tax that state levies on their purchases, regardless of whether they live in the same city or visit from across the world. That being said, if you sell the same products online, it is hard to levy a sales tax to the customers since they can place these orders from different parts of the country or globe.

If you run the business in Canada, you must collect the HST and GST of the customers, and do the same if you earn more than $30,000 in a year. You can also collect this information from customers even if you do not earn as much, and add this information to earn tax credits.

It is easier to sell to international customers because you do not have to levy a sales tax on these customers. If you run a store in Canada, you do not have to charge the customers living outside of Canada, a GST, or HST. An international purchase is tax-exempt, even for American store owners. This tax rate will differ depending on the state you live in, so it is best to check with the accountant to see if you are eligible for this exemption.

Determine the Tax Obligations

As mentioned earlier, the tax obligations of your business will vary depending on the structure. If you run a sole proprietorship, a sole partnership, or LLC, you will claim the business income when you file the personal tax return. A Corporation is a separate legal entity, and the tax rates are calculated separately from the owner's tax rates. If you earn an amount from the Corporation, you must tax it the same way an employee would tax it. A self-employed individual can withhold taxes from the income, and also remit these taxes. If you own a store in the US, you must pay an estimated quarterly tax if you owe the government more than $1000 during the fiscal year.

Calculate the Gross Margins

When you improve the gross margin of the store, you can increase your overall income. To calculate the gross margin, you must list the costs that you incur to produce the product or service. Let us define the terms cost of goods sold and gross margin to understand these better:

Cost of Goods Sold

These are the direct costs that the business will incur when it produces the products that it sells. These costs will include direct labor, material, and machinery costs.

Re-Evaluate the Methods

When you start the business, you can choose to use a simple spreadsheet to help you manage your books. When your business starts to grow, you should switch to different or more advanced methods such as Bench or QuickBooks. As the business continues to grow, you should reassess the time you spend on the books and also determine how you can use your time better. If you have the right bookkeeping solution, it means you can invest more time in your business and also save your business a lot of money.

It is overwhelming to start a business, but if you stick to the points in this chapter, you can have your finances in order right from the beginning. The tasks in this chapter will contribute to the success of your business, and they will help you when your business continues to grow.

Chapter 5: Tax Preparation

Paying taxes can seem like a herculean task to someone who is doing it for the first time. In fact, those that pay regularly will also feel like it is a demanding task where one wrong move can land you in trouble.

But don't worry; you can enlist the help of a professional tax preparer to help you prepare your taxes. Professional taxpayers can be chartered accountants or a qualified tax preparer.

Here are some aspects you must bear in mind while hiring a tax preparer.

No one size fits all

Before you start hunting for the best tax preparer, you have to understand that there will not be a standard agent who will come over and prepare your taxes. So stop asking your family and friends to suggest you the best one, as you will have to do the dirty work yourself. You have to put in efforts to find the one that will best suit your business. Start early, so that you can spend some time looking for the best person to file your taxes.

Look for PTIN

The next thing is to check whether the person has a valid preparer tax identification number. Better known as PTIN, this is a number that tells you whether the person is a qualified preparer or not. Do make it a point to ask this at the very beginning as you don't want to end up with someone who does not have the number and has yet prepared your tax papers for you.

Qualifications

The next thing is to check the qualifications of the person. Most tax preparers like to add in many alphabets next to their name to showcase their qualifications. But just a bunch of letters next to each other does not mean they are highly qualified. It can just mean they have passed a few necessary tests. It is ideal for the person to have a CFP qualification that stands for certified financial planner board of planners. You can also see if the person is a qualified lawyer with a JD or LLM.

History

Next, you have to check the tax preparer's history. You have to see if they have prepared tax forms in the past. You can ask them for a background check and see who they have worked with. You can also visit their website (if they have one) and look up testimonials. It is important for you to do your research before hiring someone, as you cannot take your taxes lightly.

How well versed?

The next thing to check is how well versed the person is with the state and city rules. Any professional tax preparer will be well versed in federal tax rules since it is universal. But, the state and city rules differ between states, which make it important for the preparer to know about them well in advance. You can ask and find out if he knows about the rules.

Providing forms

When you wish to prepare the taxes then you obviously have to provide the right documents for the taxes. You have to provide the tax preparer with Forms W-2, 1099 and 1098. These forms will contain information with regard to your incomes and expenses. You must also be ready to provide the preparer with any other information that he or she seeks. Preparing everything in advance will help you remain ready at the last minute.

Fees

Many first time tax preparer employers make the mistake of not asking how much the fees will be. In fact, that is not even the right approach to take while asking about the fees. You have to ask how the fees will be determined and on what basis you are being charged whatever you are. Fees are extremely important to settle well in advance to avoid any discrepancies later. Before you have the final word, you have to have a specific number in mind to know if you are paying the right amount. It is vital to avoid those preparers that ask you for a percentage of what you will be filing. Whether you file a large sum or a small one, you have to ultimately pay the preparer his rightful due and not any more.

Electronic filing

Remember to settle for a preparer that is well versed in electronic filing. After all, you want someone that will do his job quickly and help you finish up with all legal processes at the earliest. It is quite simple to file electronically and you can save on a lot of time and effort. If you are well versed with it but your preparer isn't, then you can assist him while he files electronically.

Audits

Next, you must ask your tax preparer if he will be ready for an audit. Everybody dreads an audit for obvious reasons, but it is best to prepare for one in advance in order to avoid issues later. If your tax preparer has faced an audit before then well and good, but if he has not, then you must ask him how you can prepare for one in advance.

Contact

You must ensure that the tax preparer is easily reachable and you can give him a call at any time of the day. It is best to ask for multiple contact details so that you can at least pursue one of them to successfully contact him.

Return copy

You have to ask your tax preparer for a copy of the tax return that was filed for you. It might take some time for the preparer to file all the papers and assemble them in the correct order, but you must ensure that you get a copy before he files it. You have to go through all the details to see if everything is fine.

Signature

It is extremely important for a tax preparer to sign the tax document. If your filed paper is not carrying a valid signature then you might be in a sticky spot. If your tax preparer is not willingly signing, then you should get him to at any cost. In fact, you might want to reconsider him if he is putting up a fight.

Advantages of filing it yourself

There are certain advantages of filing taxes by yourself. First off, nobody knows your company better than yourself, so, you will be able to file taxes best. You can start filing early and be done with it on time.

Even if it seems like a herculean task, doing it once will give you the confidence to do it every year. It will get progressively easier for you.

You can save on the fees that you have to pay the tax preparer. Most tax preparers charge a hefty sum, which will turn out to be an additional and unnecessary expense.

There are not many deductions to make you can easily file your own taxes. Many times, people don't understand what needs to be deducted from where and why. They end up forgetting something and wonder what went wrong. So, if you don't have properties, investments and other such deductions to make then you can prepare the taxes by yourself.

But remember that you have to do it by yourself if you know the basic rules and regulations of taxation. If you have been paying income tax then you will be well versed with the procedure. But if you are doing it for the first time then you will have to seek professional help.

Final word: It is better to have a professional prepare your taxes for you as that can help take a lot of load off your shoulders. Many taxpayers worry about filing their taxes and end up making mistakes. As you know, it is extremely important not to make any mistake while filing taxes and you have to be quite careful with it. If you are filing for the first time, then you must compulsorily avail help lest you end up making unnecessary mistakes.

One option that you have for paying your taxes is with an IRS-approved tax preparation service that you complete online or on your computer. These are often sold in retail stores or office supply stores and is a convenient way to complete your taxes with a computer application. There are different versions for personal tax filing, business tax filing, or both. Some software applications that you might be familiar with include H&R Block and TurboTax. This is a great way to file your taxes if you have a simple tax return where you don't claim lots of deductions or have too high of an income.

Some applications that you can use on your personal computer to complete your tax return can be submitted online and therefore require Internet access. There is also tax preparation software where you can print off your taxes and mail them to the IRS that don't require an Internet connection, but it takes longer to file your return and receive a tax refund if you qualify for one.

Software is nice because it walks you step-by-step through the process of inputting your income, deductions, and state tax information, and will double check that all of the information you've input is accurate. It's very easy to mistype something, so you have to be careful with your inputting and notice if you make any mistakes while doing your taxes so that you don't underestimate what you owe or overpay because of a simple error.

Your taxes can be submitted manually or electronically depending on what you prefer. Sending your tax information by mail takes a bit longer and requires that you send a check to a separate location, so it can be much simpler filing electronically instead. You can also give the IRS your bank information to pay your taxes electronically or to automatically deposit your tax refund after a few days of processing.

Tax day is April 15th, so you want to have your tax return sent to the IRS at that time or a little bit before. If for some reason you cannot complete your taxes before that day then you should file for an extension either electronically or by mail. With an extension you'll receive 6 additional months to file your taxes, which allows you to get all of your paperwork in order. Filing an extension by mail can be completed with Form 4868.

It's important that even when you apply for an extension, that you make some form of payment toward your taxes if you believe that you owe money. You can request additional time to pay your taxes by calling the IRS if you feel that you can come up with the money in 120 days. Otherwise you should fill out Form 9465 or Form 9465-FS, which lets you set up installment payments on your taxes and makes it easier to pay throughout the year.

If you don't like to use tax preparation software on the computer, you can always complete your taxes manually. The IRS prefers that you submit your taxes by electronically filing because it reduces the chance that there are mistakes, but tax forms can be found at your local library or post office if you would like to complete it by hand. The taxpayer package should include instructions and all of the forms that you need to complete your taxes whether you're filing a 1040, 1040A, or 1040EZ. Use a black pen while completing your taxes and input your income and any deductions that you qualify for. Make sure that everything is complete, accurate, and that you have signed and dated the tax return before mailing it. If you are worried that you haven't done everything correctly, it's a good idea to have someone else look over your calculations and reduces the chances that you'll be audited.

Mail the IRS your tax return as well as any of the additional forms that you've filled out with your taxes. Place your social security number at the bottom of each page so that in case any of your papers get separated, that your identification number is listed. You'll have a state tax return as well as a federal tax return which should go to different places, make sure to remember to put your return address on the envelope.

Once you have mailed your tax forms, then you should also make a payment if you owe money. You can have an electronic funds withdrawal remove any money that you owe from your account, which is the simplest and quickest way to pay your taxes. You can also pay with a credit or debit card, by mailing a check, by sending a money order, or by enrolling in the Electronic Federal Tax Payment System.

The same rules apply for filing an extension with a paper form if you need it. Just fill out Form 4868 before the deadline. Just remember that you shouldn't do this to delay the payment if you don't have enough money for your taxes. Instead, give the IRS a call and let them know how soon you can come up with the money to pay your taxes and complete Form 9465 if you need to pay in installments and it will take you over 120 days.

The other option that you have for completing your tax return is to have a tax professional do it for you. It's a good decision to talk to a few people who can prepare your tax return for you before hand, as they might also know significant ways to save you money later on in the year. Some people turn to certified public accountants, attorneys, or tax preparation offices to complete their tax returns, so you can start your search for the right person there.

Give all of your information to your tax professional before the filing deadline and make sure that they have your contact information in case they have any questions about the documents that you've given them. Set up a time with them when you can go over your tax return and review that everything is completed correctly. During this meeting you'll sign and date each return if everything looks good.

If you use a tax professional, make sure that you give yourself and them enough time to properly review all of your documents, and to file your taxes. If you have a complicated return, it's best to leave it in the hands of a professional who is used to completing all of the tax forms, and that knows how to set up a business to receive the maximum deduction for your taxes.

Chapter 6: LLC: Business Taxes, Tax Deductions and Payroll Taxes

A limited liability company, or "LLC," like any corporation, is a separate and distinct legal entity. This means an LLC can receive a tax identification number, open a bank account, and do business, all under their name.

What does LLC mean now that we know what it stands for? Limited liability means that its owners are typically not personally responsible for the obligations and claims of the company, which are also called members. If an LLC files for bankruptcy, members are not allowed to use personal money to pay the debts of the organization. If the company faces a lawsuit, there is no chance that the owners will forfeit their home to pay a settlement.

Nevertheless, in the eyes of the IRS, LLC taxes continue to represent a sole proprietorship or partnership. The LLC does not itself pay any income taxes; instead, the owners report profits and losses on their personal tax returns. As a company, the LLC can choose to tax itself. To do so, it must comply with corporate tax regulations and reporting standards.

Until hanging out the shingle, LLC owners must file formal documents with their state, pay a filing fee, and comply with other regulations. LLCs are required to pay an additional franchise tax in some States. Partnerships and sole proprietors are not faced with the same amount of paperwork and fees. Unlike a company, an LLC does not have inventory and is not required to hold annual meetings or maintain minutes of written meetings.

Limited liability companies offer two major advantages, both coming from other popular business structures. First, like a corporation, LLCs have business profits as pass-through. That means the LLC and the corporate profits are not paid separately.

The IRS does not view the company as a separate tax body. The revenues flow through or pass directly to the owners, instead. The earnings from the company become the wealth of the members. The representatives then file their own tax returns and pay the individual income tax.

A Limited Liability Corporation, commonly known as LLC, is a pass-through entity that transmits profits and losses to the owners. It is established by one or more individuals or organizations, called members, through a written agreement that specifies the organizational structure of the company, including provisions on management, and how profits and losses are distributed.

Generally, the IRS classifies LLCs as associations with at least two individuals, while LLCs can also choose to be classified as corporations. The LLC, known as a corporation, does not pay taxes on its own— members pay them the same way they do with partners. Revenue from the collaboration is recorded on Form 1065. In fact, the LLCs file ScheduleK-1, which specifies each member's individual revenue share. Members must report on Form 1065 earnings data on Schedule E, and file it with Form 1040.

Another alternative is to file Form 8832, requiring the IRS to be handled as a company by an LLC. An LLC formed as a C Corporation records its corporate income on Form 1120. One that acts as an S Corporation declares corporate income on Form 1120S.

Individual members of the S Corp report their income taxes on Form 1120S Schedule-K1. Most small businesses tend to form as an LLC. LLC members have two significant tax benefits: no double taxes and deductible corporate losses.

Unlike C companies, where corporate income is taxed twice— both at the corporate and individual level — LLCs are taxed only once at the individual level. That means members pay corporate income taxes on their personal tax returns in the same way a sole proprietorship or an S company does. The word "pass-through" tax treatment applies to this provision.

The advantage of owning an LLC is that you can have an infinite number of members (i.e., potential shareholders) in your LLC, making money raising and expanding your company simpler. If you have various members in your LLC, you need to set ownership percentages for each member.

You can choose, for multi-member LLCs, to be paid as a company or as a corporation C. If you choose to be paid as a corporation, then your share of business income will be listed on your personal income tax returns. You'll be subject to double taxes if you choose to be paid as a company C.

On the other hand, single-member LLCs are automatically treated as sole proprietorships.

To set up and maintain your state LLC, you can incur upfront costs. For example, small business owners pay $800 in state taxes annually to run an LLC in California–regardless of how much money the LLC gains or loses.

If you're in a state where you've got to pay annual taxes to run an LLC, so your job is to grow the business enough to account for that. For run an LLC, each state has different annual taxes, and some may not have any annual state taxes, so it's important to check before you set up your business.

But the tax benefits, pass-through income, and flexibilities in management still make LLCs a common choice. It's up to your tax situation to do your research to determine which legal entity better suits your needs.

How an LLC is Taxed

But the real issue here is tax accounting, and as such, what are the tax implications of operating an LLC? This business is a pass-through entity, resembling more of a single proprietorship than a corporation. Basically, members or owners pay income taxes on their share of the entity's profits, i.e., income tax returns are passed to the owners/members instead of the business filing and paying its own.

Just like sole proprietorships, you will include your share of the LLC's profits in your personal tax returns regardless if you pull it out or leave it in the business's account. For example, your LLC earns a taxable profit of $60,000 in 2019, and regardless of your business retains it, or you pull it out, you'll pay taxes on the entire $60,000 for that year.

You will also have to pay self-employment taxes if you are actively participating in your LLC. This includes social security and Medicare.

If you elect for a single-member LLC, you will be taxed as a sole proprietorship by the IRS. Its income will be filed under your personal tax returns.

Being the only member or owner of the LLC, you will report all income or losses of the business using Schedule C together with your 1040 tax return. And whether or not you retained the earnings for future company expansion or withdrew them for your personal use, you will need to file and pay income taxes on these.

If you elect for a multi-owner or member LLC with other business partners, it'll be taxed as a partnership. The only difference with a single-member LLC is that instead of only you are filing the business's income taxes in your personal returns, all of you will be doing so according to your share of the income, i.e., your respective distributive shares. These are set out in the operating agreement of your LLC.

For most LLCs, their operating agreements designate each member's distributive share in the company's net income under his or her percentage ownership or capital contribution. Let's say that your LLC has four members: you, Christine, Jacob, and Jenny. Of the business's $50,000 capital contributions, yours is $12,500, Christine's is $10,000,

Jacob's is $15,000, and Jenny's is $12,500. The distributive share of each member in the company's net income is 25% for you, 20% for Christine, 30% for Jacob, and 25% for Jenny.

However, members of a multi-member LLC may agree on a distributive share scheme of their choosing. It may not necessarily be according to capital contribution but based on other considerations also like responsibilities in the business's operations and the number of sales they bring into the business every year. Any allocation scheme not based on actual capital contribution is called "special allocations" these have to be in line with the IRS' rules.

But regardless of the chosen allocation scheme, each member must file and pay taxes on their proportionate share of the LLC's net income even if they choose not to withdraw their share of it from the business.

And while a multi-member LLC isn't required to pay income taxes, it still needs to file IRS form 1065, just the same one that partnerships use. Why? This informational return must guarantee that each individual LLC member is reporting and filing the right income taxes. You may think of it as a check and balance of sorts for tax authorities.

The company must give its members a Schedule K-1, which breaks down every LLC member's distributive share of profits and losses. The members need to attach this form with their individual form 1040, with their attached Schedule E.

Self-Employment Taxes

As an LLC member, you are considered a self-employed businessperson and not as an employee of the company. It will not withhold Social Security and Medicare taxes for you, but instead, you will have to estimate, pay, and file them personally. The equivalent of employment taxes for people like you are self-employment taxes.

The IRS requires that any business owner that works for or helps manage an enterprise must pay self-employment taxes based on their distributive share of the LLC's net income. But if you are not involved in managing or operating the business and have chosen to just invest the money instead, you may be exempted from paying these taxes. The rules and regulations and governing self-employment taxes are complex, but it's safe to say that if you are actively participating in the LLC's operations, you must pay self-employment taxes on your share of the net income.

You other LLC members must report self-employment taxes using Schedule SE, which you will submit annually with your 1040 tax return. Compared to employees, your self-employment taxes are practically double the amount. This is because, as a self-employed businessperson, you are both the employee and the employer. You're responsible for the contributions of both.

Deductions and Expenses

You may significantly reduce the amount of taxable income you must report to the IRS by the ducting or writing off legitimate expenses related to conducting business from your business income. Some of these include the costs of starting up the business, vehicle expenses, advertising and promotion, and travel expenses, among others. To make sure you're able to maximize tax deductions, it's always best to consult with a tax accountant.

Taxes and Fees at the State Level

Usually, individual states impose taxes on LLCs' profits pretty much the same way the Internal Revenue Service does. For example, LLCs do not pay state income taxes, but their members do via their personal tax returns. However, there are some exemptions. a few of them charge LLCs taxes on the income they make on top of the income tax their members have to pay on the same income. An example of this is the state of California, which imposes an income tax on LLCs that earn more than $250,000 annually. These income taxes can go as high as $9000.

It is not a tax on their income; other states charge LLCs annual fees such as franchise taxes, renewal fees, or annual registrations. Among such states are Delaware, California, Massachusetts, Illinois, New

Hampshire, Wyoming, and Pennsylvania. Most charge only about $100 annually except for California, Illinois, Massachusetts, and Pennsylvania, which charge $800, $300, $500, and $330, respectively, every year.

If you consider these as significant tax considerations, inquire with your state's tax or revenue Department before forming an LLC. in matters like these, you have to ensure all bases are covered.

The Effect of Corporate Taxation on LLC Taxes

Whether an LLC can be tax-beneficial for you depends on what you plan to do with the profits regularly. If you plan to keep most or all of its income in the business for future expansion, then electing for corporate taxation as an LLC will be good for you. If you want your LLC to be tax like a corporation, i.e., a flat corporate tax rate, you can elect to do so by filing IRS Form 8832 and check the box on the form, which indicates "corporate treatment." After electing for this tax treatment, the profits you leave in the company will be taxed using the corporate tax rate, and you, as an owner, need not pay personal income taxes on them.

Depending on the average annual income of your LLC, corporate tax rates may lead to lower taxes. This is because corporate tax rates are flat, while personal income tax rates increase as the income also increases. To get a clear picture of the most likely tax scenario, you should check with a professional tax accountant if you elect corporate taxation. This is especially because doing so locks it up as a corporate taxpayer for the next five taxable years. You cannot go back to pass-through taxation if you regret the change within the said time frame. And even if you decide to do so after the five years are over, you and your business may experience tax consequences. Again, the importance of thinking very carefully about electing for corporate taxation cannot be overemphasized.

Payroll Tax

If you've ever earned a paycheck, then you've probably noticed a part of your salary will be taken out for different taxes. What you don't know is that your company even pays taxes on its income from its wallet. Such taxes are called taxes on payrolls.

Payroll tax is a multitude of taxes paid by the employer and sometimes deducted from paycheck by an employee. The employer then remits those taxes to the tax authority concerned.

There are numerous types of taxes on payrolls including

1. Federal income tax deductions
2. Tax on Social Security deduction
3. Tax on Medicare withheld
4. Optional withheld Medicare tax
5. State income tax deduction
6. Different local tax deductions (city, state, school district)

If your company has paid employees, you will be responsible for funding and filing work taxes. This includes taxes on Social Security and Medicare, withheld federal income tax, Federal Unemployment Tax (FUTA), and State Unemployment tax.

According to the Social Security Administration, social security taxes are 4 percent on wages paid up to $137,700 for 2020. Employers pay half, 6.2 percent, of this sum, while the other half is deducted from the salaries of the employee. The tax is broken down between employer and employee. The FUTA limit is 6.2 percent of an employee's first $7,000 you spend.

State tax thresholds for unemployment vary by state, and the size of the business, age, sector, past turnover, employee tax rates of the country, and how many workers have applied for state unemployment compensation.

If you have workers, it is your responsibility to pay payroll taxes on their salaries. Payroll taxes include withholding tax on federal income, social security and Medicare taxes, and taxes on national and state unemployment. Most companies hire a payroll firm to file tax forms on their behalf and handle their payroll tax liabilities.

Employers record payroll to arrive at net pay by measuring gross monthly wage earnings and various payroll deductions. While that sounds fairly straight on the surface, estimating miscellaneous payroll deductions allows you to be detail-oriented and to work with extreme precision.

Put, payroll taxes are taxes levied on employers ' salaries and benefits. Such revenues are used to finance social insurance programs like Social Security and Medicare. Such social insurance taxes make up 23.05 percent of the total federal, state, and local government income–the second largest source of government revenue in the United States, according to recent research by the Tax Foundation.

The majority of those social insurance taxes are the two federal payroll taxes that appear on your pay stub as FICA and MEDFICA. The first is a tax of 12.4 percent to finance social security, and the second is a tax of 2.9 percent to fund Medicaid, for a total of 15.3 percent. Half of the payroll taxes (7.65 percent) are paid directly by employers, while the other half (7.65 percent) were taken out of the paychecks for employees. Some of the best-kept payroll tax secrets might be that employees pay almost all of the payroll tax, rather than sharing the burden with their employers.

This is because the frequency of taxes is decided not by statute but by the markets. Nonetheless, the person who is required to pay the federal government a tax is often different from the person bearing the tax burden. The marketplace typically determines how the tax burden is divided between buyers and sellers, depending on which group is more sensitive to price changes (economists call this "relative price elasticity"). It turns out that labor supply–that is, the willingness of the workforce to work–is much less prone to taxes than demand for labor–or the willingness of employers to hire. This is because employees who need a job are not as sensitive to salary increases, but companies can "pick around" for the best employees or move production to different locations. The table below shows approximately how the payroll tax burden is spread on the labor market. The idea that the labor supply line is steeper than the demand line is a way of showing employees are less prone to wage increases than employers are.

Besides the fact that the implementation of "employer-side" payroll taxes by the federal government is unfair, it also contributes to a possible problem: it hides the costs of the services for which payroll taxes are paid. That is, instead of reporting the regular taxpayers ' share of Social Security and Medicare benefits directly, half of the taxes that fund the services are withheld from jobs, in the form of lower salaries.

This is a concern because it contradicts the concept of tax transparency: a tenet that specifies that tax obligations in complex structures should not be shielded from taxpayers. Since roughly half of the payroll taxes financed by Social Security and Medicare are concealed in the form of lower wages, rather than explicitly written down on our pay stubs, voters may underestimate the exact budgetary effect of these social programs.

Chapter 7: Sole Proprietorship: Business Taxes, Tax Deductions and Payroll Taxes

One of the simplest forms of business structures is the sole proprietorship. This is not a type of legal entity, but only refers to the individual who owns the business, and he is personally responsible for every individual who invests in the business. He is also solely responsible for paying off any debts incurred by the business. You can operate a sole proprietorship under the name of the owner or even an alias or fictitious name. The latter is only a trade name, and it does not separate the business from the owner. Remember, there is no way to legally separate the business from the owner.

Most businesses choose the sole proprietorship business entity form since it is extremely simple. It is easy to set it up, and there aren't too many costs associated with this business structure. A sole proprietor must only register his name and secure any required local licenses from the state. Once he does this, he is ready for business. One of the biggest disadvantages of a sole proprietorship is that the owner will remain personally liable for any business debts. If the business was to run into financial trouble, a creditor could sue the owner. If the creditor wins this lawsuit, the owner has to pay the debts with his money.

The owner of a business following the sole proprietorship structure will sign contracts in his name since the business does not have a separate identity. The owner can request the customers to write any checks in his name, even if the business has a different name. These owners can mix business property and funds with their personal funds, and other business structures are not allowed to do this. The business owner can also have a bank account in his name if he uses this business structure.

The owner of a sole proprietorship does not have to observe any formalities such as meetings or voting associated with complex business forms; he can make all or any major decisions as per his or her own will. The owner can sue creditors or customers using his name. Most businesses start off as sole proprietorships and slowly graduate or move to complex business forms.

Since it is difficult to distinguish between the sole proprietorship business and the owner, it is extremely simple to complete the taxes for the business. The income the business earns is the same as the income the owner earns. A sole proprietorship will report the income losses and expenses by filing Schedule C and form 1040. You will record the profits and losses first in Schedule C, which is a tax form, and file that along with Form 1040. You will then transfer the final amount from Schedule C to the personal tax return forms. This is an attractive aspect since the losses your business suffers will offset any income you earn from other sources.

As the sole proprietor, you should file Schedule SE along with Form 1040. Using this form, you can calculate the amount of tax you owe to the government for self-employment. You do not have to pay any employment tax for yourself, but if you have employees in your business, you must pay that on their behalf. You will not enjoy any benefits if the business suffers.

As mentioned earlier, this type of proprietor is personally liable for any debts of the business. Let's understand this better because the idea of personal liability is scary. Let us assume that you borrow money from investors and the bank to operate, and soon you lose some of your major customers. When you start losing money, you can either file for bankruptcy or work until your business runs out of money. You cannot repay the loan that you took from the bank. Now, the bank can seize or come after your personal assets to recover the loan.

Consider a worst-case scenario. Your business is involved in an accident that injured or killed someone. The family can file a negligence lawsuit against your business. Remember, they can file the suit against you and your personal assets, such as your retirement account, home, and bank account. Consider these situations carefully before you choose the sole proprietorship business structure. Accidents will happen, and your business can no longer be held responsible. If your business should suffer unfortunate circumstances as mentioned above, it can become a nightmare for you.

If another party or employee from your business were to wrong someone you do business with, the victim party could file a lawsuit against your (business owner's) name. If the business structure was a Corporation or LLC, the entity bringing the claim should bring it against the name of the company. The advantages of a sole proprietorship are:

• The owner can establish a business easily and instantly. It will not cost them too much

• A sole proprietorship will carry very few ongoing formalities

• A business using this structure does not have to pay any unemployment tax for himself

• The owner can mix personal and business assets

The disadvantages of this business structure are:

• The owner is personally liable for the losses, liabilities, and debts of the business

• The owner can raise capital by selling the business idea to investors and banks

• Most sole proprietorship owners cannot survive the incapacity or death of their owners and do not retain any value

One of the greatest features of the sole proprietorship is that it is simple to form. You only need to spend a little more to buy and sell different materials, goods, and services. You do not have to even formally file any documents to form the sole proprietorship.

Small Business Taxes for Sole Proprietors

A small business can calculate its business profit or laws using income taxes. It can then include this information on its personal tax returns. This chapter will shed some light on the different forms you must use to compile the information for the IRS if you follow the sole proprietorship business structure.

Due Dates

Since every small business will file its tax returns the same day as the personal returns, the due dates are the same as the personal income tax due date mentioned above. If this due date falls on a weekend or a holiday, the business day after April 15th is the due date.

- Should I hire a professional to work on my taxes?

Most small businesses need a tax preparer unless they have no assets to depreciate or cost of goods sold. In the case of the latter situation, the business can use a tax software program. It is complicated to file income taxes for a partnership, corporation, and even a simple Schedule C. Understand the different types of taxes and what you must look out for before you enlist the help of a qualified tax preparer, enrolled agent or CPA.

Schedule C Income Tax Forms

If you follow the sole proprietor business structure or a single-member LLC, you will need to file the following forms to calculate the self-employment tax:
- Schedule C
- Schedule C Instructions
- Schedule SE to calculate the self-employment tax
- Schedule SE instructions

Details to Complete Schedule C

You need the following information if you want to complete the schedule C form.
- You must calculate the cost of goods sold if you maintain an inventory of parts or products.
- If you deduct any amounts from the taxable income, you must provide sufficient evidence, including information on driving expenses, business travel, and business meals. Remember, any business entertainment expenses are no longer deductible as an expense from the taxable income.

- You must also include information on the cost you incur when you buy business assets, such as the vehicles and equipment. You also need to calculate any depreciation on these assets.
- If you work from home, include information on how you use your house to conduct business.

Self-Employment Taxes

A small business owner has to pay self-employment taxes. These taxes include Medicare and Social Security taxes. You can use a software program or take the help of a tax preparer to calculate the amount for you. Alternatively, you can calculate this amount yourself using the schedule SE.

Adding Schedule C to the Personal Tax Return

Your net business income online 31 in the schedule C form is added to the personal income tax return form. Any other business adjustments or tax credits you can receive must be included in the adjusted gross income section in your personal income tax form. You should include half the self-employment tax liability to the adjusted gross income section. You should enter the self-employment tax you owe from the schedule SE to line 57 in your personal income tax return form.

How to File Schedule C

You can file your tax return online or email it to the state. The last page of the instructions will list the addresses you can Mail the tax form. If you use tax software, you can include the e-filing option by paying a small fee. If you use a tax preparer to help you with filing your taxes, include this cost to the amount you pay the tax preparer.

Filing an Application for Extension

You can apply for an automatic extension of the time given to file your taxes. This extension is for a period of six months for non-corporate tax returns; therefore, the due date will now be October 15th. Remember, an extension of the due date will not extend the payment due date. You must pay the tax due to the government on April 15th.

Special Filing Cases

If you and your partner own the business, you can file a qualified joint venture form. This means you will file two Schedule C forms, one for your business and one for yourself. This is a complicated method to follow; therefore, check with your tax professional before you do this. Remember to determine if you qualify for this filing method.

Chapter 8: IRS: Dealing With the IRS, Remaining in Good Standing With the IRS, How to

Tips to Avoid IRS Audits

For a small business, it is nothing short of a nightmare to be audited by the IRS. If your business doesn't file its taxes on time, underpays the estimated taxes, or miscalculates taxes, it will all attract the attention of the IRS. In case of an IRS audit, you might be asked to produce all receipts for the last five years of your business. You'll probably want to look at all your books of accounts, if you don't have all these receipts in order, the books of accounts are not in order, or if you don't have a detailed record of all the receipts and income. All this will only worsen the situation the business is already in and make your business seem like it's evading its tax responsibilities.

Fortunately, this nightmare doesn't necessarily have to turn into a reality for your business. Only a small number of small businesses tend to get audited for tax evasion. Also, before your business is audited, the IRS usually sends a letter asking for documentation that helps clear up any discrepancies found in tax filings. Regardless of all this, it is never in your business's good interests to be audited by the IRS. In this section, let's look at simple steps every small business owner can follow to avoid an IRS audit.

Reporting Losses

If your business reports a net loss for more than two out of the five consecutive years, it can trigger the scrutiny of the IRS. So, if you don't want to make your business seem like an ideal candidate for a tax audit, ensure that your business stays profitable. Well, this is an obvious motive for any business owner. If your business incurs net losses for two years, then the IRS might determine your business is not really a business, but it is a hobby. If the business is deemed to be a hobby, then all the deductions applicable to business expenses will soon disappear from your income tax returns.

No Excess Payments

A corporation is believed to have a separate entity than that of its shareholders. Make it a point that the business never overpays salaries to employees who are also shareholders of the business. If a C-corporation pays exceptionally high salaries to its executives, it is viewed as a technique used to minimize corporate profits. If the corporate profits shown by the business are low, then the tax payable by it also automatically reduces. It, in turn, can seem like tax evasion to the IRS. This is one reason why the IRS can scrutinize the income tax returns filed by a Corporation because of extremely high salary payments. Payment of salaries to employees is different from the salaries payable to employees who are also the shareholders in the business.

Check the Numbers

If you receive a tax form to report income, such as the Form 1099, then keep in mind that the party who issues it also files the same form with the IRS. It is quite obvious that the IRS would expect the numbers to match both these forms. For instance, if your business claims that it received $ 5000 for services provided, then the receiver of such service also files a similar form, which states that he paid $5000 for services provided by your business. So, in this case, the numbers match, and if these numbers don't match, it looks like a red flag to the IRS. Any discrepancy in these reports and the IRS might issue your business notice or even audit the tax returns filed by a business.

If the numbers do not add up on your tax returns, it's quite likely that it calls for an IRS audit. Mistakes are incredibly easy to make, and there can be some unchecked mistakes present in the final forms filed for the business. Therefore, make a point of always double-checking all the information in the income tax returns, make sure you check the numbers as well. The best way to avoid any unnecessary mistakes in this regard is to use tax software, or maybe even hire a tax preparer. Even calculation mistakes can lead to discrepancies, which are regularly flagged by the IRS.

Estimated Taxes

If you believe that your business owes at least $500 as taxes by the end of the year, ensure that it pays its estimated taxes on time. Every small business is required to make a quarterly estimated tax payment. If your business fails to make such payments or makes inadequate payments, it becomes a red flag for the IRS. Any failure to make such payments can incur penalties for your business and increase its risk of a tax audit by the IRS. It's quite simple to calculate the estimated taxes. You merely need to go through the income tax returns of the previous year and 100% of such taxes. It's always better to overpay or estimate taxes, then underpay them. However, when you do overpay, you should not go overboard.

Legitimate Deductions

There are plenty of deductions a small business can claim. From home office expenses to vehicles used for any out of town business purposes, they are all deductible expenses. Ensure that every deduction you include is a legitimate one. The deduction should be fair and not over the top. A common mistake a lot of small business owners make is that they make illegitimate claims for their home office deduction. Home offices are usually viewed as red flags for any tax audit. However, if the space you use qualifies for a deduction, you have nothing to worry about.

A home office should be used exclusively for your business, and it needs to be a separate room. If you place a desk in the corner of your living room and claim it to be your home office, it doesn't work. If the expenses incurred by the business for the maintenance of the home office are quite high, or the deductions made for the home office expenses are high, it is seen as a red flag. Never claim the expenses for a home office if your business rents an office space elsewhere. You cannot claim both these deductions at the same time when they are associated with the same expense- office space for the business.

When it comes to deductions, they certainly help reduce the overall tax burden. Deductions and tax credits are quite helpful. A tax credit reduces your tax payable, whereas a deduction helps reduce the overall taxable income. Keep in mind that certain deductions cannot be claimed when a tax credit is used and vice versa. Therefore, take some time out of your schedule and go through the list of deductions and tax credits available for small businesses. Whenever you find something that seems to apply to your business, make a note of it. Also, ensure that you do all of this at the beginning of the tax year itself. If you wait until the end to use all these things, your business will lose out on more money than it makes. For instance, when you are aware since the beginning that your small business is eligible for a home office deduction, you can make the most of a home office.

Accurate Records

If you want to reduce the chances of an IRS audit for the business, ensure that you maintain good records. Your business needs to maintain records of not just the expenses it incurs, but also all the income it receives along the way. This tip is applicable to not just the year-end tax filing season, but for everything else, your business does throughout the year. The importance of maintaining good and clear records can never be underestimated.

Make it a point that the business always has a separate bank account, and this bank account is never used for any personal purposes. Likewise, your personal accounts should not be used for business purposes. Even if there are any overlapping expenses, make a detailed note of it, and keep the records separate. If you do use the personal account for business purposes or the business account for private purposes, keep records of such receipts and payments.

The risk of your business getting audited by the IRS increases when there is no proper record of all income and expenses. Also, if your business doesn't report them properly, it incurs the unwarranted attention of the IRS. If your business tries to hide its income or overstate its expenses actively, then it is considered to be tax evasion. There are various international tax shelters, which can be used. Not just foreign, but even domestic tax shelters are quite helpful for small businesses. However, be careful about how your business uses all this. Whenever in doubt, seek professional help. Do you remember the age-old saying, "A stitch in time saves nine?" If yes, then this is the motto you should live by when it comes to taking care of your business records.

Independent Contractors

If a business has a high ratio of independent contractors to employees, then it is seen as a red flag. Whenever a business has employees, then it is liable to pay salaries to them. Apart from salaries, the business is also liable to pay payroll taxes. If it hires an independent contractor, then it doesn't have to pay payroll taxes. Therefore, it's a common practice for small businesses to avoid paying payroll taxes by employing a lot of independent contractors. Therefore, ensure that the ratio of independent contractors hired by the business is not too high. There are a couple of guidelines issued by the IRS about the services of individuals who can be considered to be an independent contractor for a concerned business. You should go through the rules that differentiate between those who can be deemed to be employees and independent contractors. Ensure that your business follows all these rules. Whenever in doubt, seek immediate help from a tax professional to ensure that your business doesn't make any costly mistakes.

Report Income and Expenses

Usually, it's a common practice for taxpayers to round off the numbers to the nearest dollar. For instance, if it is $4.95, it is acceptable to round it off as $5. However, it is far from acceptable if your business rounds off $4900 as $5000. Never round numbers to the nearest tens or hundreds. It might give the impression to the IRS that your business is effectively overstating its expenses.

The simplest way for a business to avoid an IRS audit is to file its taxes on time. Your business should do this, not just accurately but also with integrity. If you follow all the steps as mentioned earlier in this section, it's quite likely that you can avoid any accidental triggers that bring your business under the scrutiny of the IRS. So, take some time and try to implement all the different tips discussed in the section. They are not only simple to follow but also practical. Instead of slowing down your business operations later, it's better to pause right now and ensure that everything is in order.

IRS Audit Process

An IRS audit or even an audit, in general, is nothing more than a second look. In an IRS audit, the auditor merely takes another look at the tax return filed by the business for a given year. There are several factors like the ones discussed above, which can increase the risk of your business being audited, but most of the IRS audits are usually random. The IRS generally selects a couple of tax returns every year to conduct a compliance check. So, an audit, in this sense, is quite similar to a quality control measure you might use in your business.

Audits can be conducted in person or through correspondence. Most of the audits are often initiated within two years of the date from which you file your taxes. However, if the IRS feels like there are any substantial errors in the taxes your business has been filing, then it can go back to up to 6 years. The most common type of audit that small businesses are subjected to is known as a correspondence audit. In this audit, a notification is given by the IRS to a small business in writing, informing the owner about an issue, or any mistake present in the tax return of the business. A business is required to respond in writing with additional support and documentation as proof for any of the apparent mistakes in the report.

A field audit is when an auditor comes to the place of business and conducts a thorough audit. However, this type of audits is not as common as correspondence audits. In both situations, ensure that you engage a business attorney with a specialization in business tax matters. The notices which are given to the business for an IRS audit include the contact information of the concerned auditor, instructions on the steps the business needs to follow, and a detailed list of all the documents or information the auditor wants to examine.

Once you follow these instructions, ensure that you carefully organize and compile all the information the IRS auditor needs from your business. During an audit, the auditor tends to compare the tax returns for the year under scrutiny with the books of your business in a concerned year. Ensure that the financial statements such as the balance sheet, profit or loss statement, and any other documents that you used to prepare the books of accounts are in order. Also, ensure that these numbers match the ones stated in your tax returns.

Keep in mind that the auditor's job is to go through all the books to ensure there are no errors on the tax return for the year in which your business is audited.

Outcomes of an IRS Audit

An IRS audit can have any of the following outcomes.

Verification of Information

If the IRS auditor goes through all the business information and finds that everything is in order, you don't have to worry about any changes to the tax return. Keep in mind that the auditor will go through all your books of records, will ask for additional documents whenever required, and even verify the records of receipts and payments made by the business. Don't be hesitant, and you certainly don't have to worry about all these things. As long as everything is in order, you can rest easy.

Any Dispute About a Mistake

The auditor finds errors, and you don't agree with these errors. If there is any dispute about any findings, then you have up to 30 days to file an appeal to the IRS. You can do this even if the auditor's findings are not in your favor or if his findings are wrong, and you are aware of it. You also have the option to suit the IRS in the court of law.

Keep in mind that if your business gets caught evading taxes or indulging in any tax fraud, then the penalties can be quite high. If there is any mistake on your tax return and the auditor finds it, it's a good idea to ask a tax attorney to assess the issue before you do anything else.

Dealing with a Mistake

The second outcome is that the auditor finds certain errors, and you acknowledge these errors. If you acknowledge the errors, it means you are liable to pay the additional taxes required and any other penalties or interest on the additional amount payable. If you miscalculated your taxes and paid more than you were supposed to, then you are eligible for a refund.

Should a Business Worry

A common concern that keeps up small business owners at night is the thought of their business getting audited by the IRS. There are many uncertainties and challenges a business owner needs to face, such as making the required number of sales, attracting and holding onto new clients, and even dealing with difficult business situations. Apart from all these things, as a business owner, you also need to ensure that your business makes timely and accurate tax payments. Worrying about an IRS audit is quite common, but it should not be your primary fear. Even if it is an unpleasant experience, as long as your books are in order and you have paid your taxes properly, you have nothing to worry about. As long as you have not deliberately underreported the business income, exaggerated its expenses, or claimed any inaccurate deductions, you can rest easy. An IRS audit is a routine procedure.

Instead of worrying about the audit, ensure that your business takes the required steps to avoid such an audit. The simplest thing you can do is accurately record and report the business income and expenses every year. Don't be hesitant to hire an accountant or a tax professional when the need arises. Always use a reliable tax preparation software to avoid any clerical or manual errors. If your business follows the tips discussed in this chapter, it can significantly reduce the chances of an IRS audit.

Chapter 9: Keep Good Records, What to Keep and For How Long

In addition to helping you keep track of the financial information for your business, doing well with your bookkeeping can help you get prepared when it is time for tax season. Many new business owners feel a bit overwhelmed when it is time to do their taxes. But if you have maintained your books through the year, then tax time is going to be easy.

There are a few things that you need to know before filing your federal income tax. As a small business, you may make the mistake of thinking the IRS is not concerned with your tax liability. However, the IRS does care quite a bit. This chapter will take a look at some of the things that you should watch out for when it comes to working on your taxes.

The Legal Entity You Choose Can Affect Your Tax Burden

Your small business may not have to shoulder the same tax burden that another one does. The legal entity that you go with can have a bit effect on the amount of tax liability that you have throughout the years.

There are different types of entities that your business can choose. You can be a sole proprietorship, an LLC or an S corporation to name a few. The S corporation is beneficial because it allowed you the advantage of being able to pay your taxes at the same level as a shareholder, but it does limit how many stocks you can use. The C corporation can help you deduct more expenses at tax time, but it includes double taxation and a lot more paperwork compared to others.

You should carefully look through your business and decide which of these entities is the best one for your needs. Each one has a benefit and some negatives, so you want to look through them all to make sure that you pick out the best one for your needs.

You Can Sometimes Deduct More Than You Think

As a small business, you are probably used to having to stretch out your budget as far as possible. You may not have the stockholders to rely on and you certainly don't have the large budget that some of the capital that the bigger companies should have. Despite this smaller business budget, you still need to pay for raw materials, rent for the building you use, the salaries of any employees you hire, the operational costs, and even utilities. The good news is that a small business owner is able to deduct many of these expenses and lower their tax burdens so they can stretch their business profits further.

There are a lot of expenses that can fall into this and that you are able to deduct when it is tax season. You can deduct the rent on your home office or business, computers, office equipment, supplies, and more. In addition, small businesses can deduct the costs that they pay when providing healthcare benefits to any employees. You should take the time to research all of the deductions that apply to you to help save money and lessen your tax bill.

It is important that you go through all the deductions and see if they pertain to you. This is one of the best ways to help you save money on the amount that you pay in taxes. You can then put this money back into your business and see it grow some more.

Remember Those Startup Expenses

One mistake that a new startup will make is thinking that the expenses they incur for starting a business can't be deducted. However, the IRS will allow small business owners to deduct quite a few of their startup expenses, even the ones that occur before they open their doors.

Although the expenses for starting up a business will differ depending on the industry, most businesses could deduce any investigational costs they incur when analyzing products and researching the market for their product. You can deduce costs for training employees, going to trade shows, locating suppliers, and even advertising to your potential employees.

One thing to note here is that you can only deduct the expenses that lead to the creation of a viable business entity. If you decide, after going through these expenses, not to form the business, then these costs become personal expenses, and it is possible that none of them will be deductible.

If you want to claim some of the expenses that you incurred while opening the business, you must keep good records ahead of time. This will make it easier to prove these expenses at tax time. If you keep them all organized through the year, it will also save you time having to search through everything later to find this information.

Make the Estimated Payments

As a new business owner, you probably know how important it is for you to pay your taxes accurately and on time. However, many self-employed persons are also responsible for making estimated tax payments each quarter through the year.

During your first year of operation, you are excused from making these estimated tax payments. However, you are still responsible for doing it in the second year and onwards. Business owners who file as sole proprietors or a partner in the S-corporation must all start making estimated tax payments any time they anticipate that they will owe $1,000 or more for that tax year.

You Must Pay the Self-Employment Tax

For those who are brand new to owning a business, you may not be sure what the self-employment tax is all about. This tax is comprised of the Medicare and Social Security taxes and it is owed by anyone who doesn't have employer withholding on them. Since you are self-employed and don't have your own employer any longer, you will be responsible for both your own portion and the portion that is usually paid by an employer to satisfy this tax.

To help ease their burden a little bit when it comes to tax time, you should try to deduct the employer-equivalent component of their self-employment tax. Doing this, and making sure that you claim all the right deductions will ensure that you are able to keep this tax as low as possible at the end of the year.

Claiming all the business expenses that you have will do wonders to helping you limit the amount that you need to pay during tax time. You can work with your accountant to figure out which of these, and other deductions, you can use to help keep more money in your pocket during tax time.

How to Prepare W2's for Your Employees

If you have employees in your business, you will need to know how to prepare a W2. When you hire a new employee, you need to ask them to fill out a W4 for a regular employee, or a W9 for an independent contractor. You will need this information to help you prepare your W2s.

The W4 form needs to be on file with the business the whole time that the employee works with you. If there are changes that you need to make to this file, such as when an employee moves, then you need to have them fill out a new form. Before preparing the W2, make sure that all your employees take a look at their W4 to ensure that the information is up to date and accurate.

You will need to get all the information that the W2 requires. This will include the social security number of the employee (so it matches up when they do taxes), their name, address, how much they made and so on. Once you have all this information, you can then review and create your W2s.

Any employee who works for you at some point during the year will need to get a W2 from your business. It doesn't matter if they only worked for a few months or if they quit at the beginning of the year, or anything else. If they worked even one day for you during that fiscal year, then they need to get a W2.

There are several methods that you can use to get the W2 forms ready for printing. You can get them directly from the IRS, use a tax or accounting software, ask your CPA, or even purchase them from a local office supply store. When it comes to getting them from the IRS website, you are not able to directly download it from the site.

If you have the capabilities of doing this, an accounting software that has a payroll feature can help. You can just add this on and the work will be done with you. The accounting software can keep track of all the information for the year and then you just need to go through it and ensure the information is accurate before you print it off.

Next, you need to distribute the W2s so that your employees are able to use them on their own tax returns. You must get these to your employees by January 31st at the latest. You can either send out these out through the mail or you can have your employees pick them up. Some businesses are also choosing to have these documents available on a secured website to make it easier on everyone and to ensure that all the employees have a copy, won't lose it, and will get the information in time.

Once the employees all have their W2s, it is time to figure out how you are going to file them with the Social Security Administration. You need to file form W-3 complete with a copy A of each W2 for your employees. Two other methods you can use to file these forms include:

- File online at the business services online section of the Social Security website. You will need to go through some registration steps to file this electronically.
- Mail completed forms of W2 and W3 to the Social Security Administration

If you are in a state where the employee needs to pay their state taxes, then copy 1 of the W2 needs to be sent to the state taxing authority for each state that the employee worked in and paid taxes to.

Record the Deposits Correctly

The reason that this one is so important is that it makes it less likely that you are going to pay taxes on money that isn't income. You never want to pay more taxes than you need to, especially when it comes to paying it on money that isn't your income.

The best thing here is to take up a system that will keep all the financial activities of your business straight, whether it is a notebook that you use on a regular basis, the help of an Excel spreadsheet, or some software that can record all of your financial information.

As a business owner, you will need to make a wide variety of deposits into your bank account throughout a fiscal year, including deposits about revenue from any sales, cash infusions from the personal savings, or loans. The trouble here is that when the year ends, you (or a bookkeeping you decide to work with), might go through this information and then record some of the deposits as income when they aren't your income. And when this happens, you could end up paying taxes on more money than what you actually made that year.

Set Money Aside to Help You Pay for Your Taxes

If you are past your first year of business, or you are a sole proprietorship who owed the IRS $1,000 or more for a year, then you need to file quarterly tax returns. If you fail to do this, then the IRS could levy interest and penalties for not filing these on time.

The best thing to do here is to systematically put some of the money aside during the year that you can use to pay your taxes. Then, on the calendar, you will note the deadlines for the taxes, along with any preparation time if it is needed. This ensures that you are actually able to make the tax payments to the IRS on time when they are due.

One thing that can be especially problematic for your business is the payroll taxes. There are times when some entrepreneurs, who aren't taking care of their finances properly, will be crash-crunched and end up in a down cycle. They will dip into the employee withholdings, the money that was earmarked to be sent to the IRS.

Keep a Tab on the Invoices That You Have

You will quickly find in your business that any late bills or unpaid bills are going to cut into the cash flow that you have. When people are not paying the invoice that they owe to you, and you had to pay for employees to do the work and materials, this can really end up putting you behind. You had to pay for everything upfront and now you have to make due and keep getting things paid upfront for other customers, without having that money from the original customers.

You have to always keep track of the invoices that you have to make sure they are all paid on time. It is important to assign someone in your company to keep track of your billing. Then put a process in place so that you can make phone calls, send out a second invoice, and levying penalties, such as extra fees at a certain deadline.

When it comes to the invoices that you have, you want to make sure that you have a plan in place in case one of your customers doesn't pay their bill to you yet, since this can influence the cash flow so much. Come up with a plan of what you will need to do if the customer is 30, 60, or 90 days late on an invoice that you sent them.

Chapter 10: Common Business Tax Mistakes and FAQs

It is the responsibility of every business to file its tax returns regularly without fail. Certain tax mistakes can prove to be quite expensive, and others attract unnecessary penalties from IRS audits to penalties and interest. You can save yourself and your business a lot of unnecessary grief if you are careful while filing taxes.

When it comes to taxes, the best way to learn is through experience. However, you don't always have to make mistakes to learn. You can learn a lot from the mistakes that others make as well. In this section, let us look at some common tax mistakes you need to avoid.

It is your business's responsibility to report its income for all the goods and services it has sold and rendered. If your business purchased any goods and services, the transaction is taxable for the business. Regardless of whether a set of goods were exchanged for another set or not, the transaction should be recorded.

These days, most businesses conduct transactions using virtual currency. So, if your business gets paid or pays virtual currency for goods or services, the transactions need to be reported. Keep in mind that the IRS monitors all virtual currency transactions. Any failure to adequately report the income or misreporting the income will lead to penalties.

Regardless of the entity or type of business, certain transactions associated with income will be reported by your business, such as form 1099 MISC that shows compensation for nonemployees or 1099K, which is used for credit cards and other transactions. The IRS closely monitors all the transactions that are reported by businesses. Therefore, it is a business's obligation to pick up the information correctly and then transmit the same through the applicable tax forms.

If your business uses the wrong forms, you don't send them on time, or you report the wrong amount, then it can incur various tax penalties.

Never misreport the income and expenses of a business if you don't want to end up in any legal trouble.

Keep in mind that only 50% of certain business meals can be included as deductible expenses. Even if you are out of town on a legitimate business trip or pay for the meals of a customer who does business with you, only 50% of these transactions can be claimed as deductions. You can never claim 100% of these transactions. Remember that all deductions have certain limitations, and if you exceed such limitations, it can cause legal trouble.

Another common income tax mistake is over-reporting the income earned by a business. If your business sells inventory items, consider the cost of goods sold, so that your business doesn't pay tax on the gross receipts from the sales made. The income earned by the business is the difference between the cost of the item and the amount you get from the sale of the item.

A cardinal sin you must avoid when it comes to taxes is to combine the business expenses with personal ones. Keep in mind that there needs to be a separate account and record for both these transactions. You must never mix them. If you wrongly charge or classify any personal transactions as business transactions, it can be deemed to be a fraudulent transaction by the IRS. If you endlessly treat personal income as business revenue, you might end up paying more taxes than required. Regardless of whether it is a sole proprietorship, a partnership, or even a limited liability company, ensure that there are separate bank accounts, credit cards, and debit cards for your personal and business use.

As a taxpayer and a business owner, keep in mind that if you have a home office, then you can deduct the expenses that go toward the maintenance of such an office. As long as you stick to the conditions and regulations laid down by the IRS, you can always deduct the expenses associated with a home office. A common misconception is that owners of small businesses wrongly believe that any deduction relating to the home office is considered to be an audit red flag.

If your personal vehicle is used for business purposes, ensure that you maintain separate records for such use. If you don't, then you are not entitled to make a deduction for the business expense that was incurred through your personal resources. Record keeping is an extremely important aspect of your business, and unless you do it properly, you cannot claim the necessary deductions. If you cannot claim such deductions, then your business is essentially losing money where it could have saved some.

There are certain tax credits a business stands to gain. One important tax credit is appropriate utilization of retirement plans. Any contributions made by a business toward retirement and its employee's plan can be treated as a deductible expense. Also, it helps the business on certain tax credits. Carefully consider the pros and cons of each of the options available and select one route.

A common mistake made by several business owners is that they claim deductions and tax credits for the same transactions. As mentioned in the previous point, if you claim a deduction for the contribution made to an employee's insurance, then the same transaction cannot be treated as a tax credit. You can either opt for a tax credit or a business deduction and not both for a single transaction. If your business claims both these options, then it can be termed as misrepresentation of income.

Any start-up costs incurred by the business during the first year can be deducted. All expenses that the business incurred before its doors were open for business are deductible expenses. Up to $5,000 can be deducted as start-up costs. If your business fails to do this within the first year of business, you cannot claim this tax deduction ever again.

Pass-through entities and S Corporation's shareholders and partners can be claimed on personal returns, but this claim is restricted to a certain basic amount. For instance, for the owners' loss in S Corporation, the deduction is limited to the stock he owns, and the loan given by him to the S Corporation. If there are no records of such stockholding certificates or loans the owner has made to the Corporation, then he cannot claim the losses as an expense. Likewise, any capital gain from the sale of business property is not the entire amount that is received from the proceeds. In fact, it is the difference between the sales proceeds and the basis in the property. The basis is the cost spent to acquire the property, and it is further reduced by depreciation.

Businesses can make charitable donations and claim them as tax deductions. However, if more than $250 is paid by the business as a charitable donation, then there needs to be an acknowledgment for the same. If there is no proper record of such donations or if donations are not made to legitimate charities, then there are no tax breaks available.

There are different carryovers such as investment interest, capital losses, net operating losses, deductions for home, office, or even general business credits. Some businesses have the option to write off losses from prior years in their current year. If you don't check for such carryovers, you cannot use them later. There is a time limit applicable for every carryover depending on the kind of expense it is based on. So, carefully go through the list of carryovers and use the ones that are applicable to your business.

One tax mistake you must never make if you want to be a legitimate business is to maintain dishonest and inaccurate employee records. If you fudge the worker records or treat full-time employees as freelancers or contractors, your business can land in unnecessary legal trouble. Even if it stands to gain some simple reductions in tax rates, it is not in the best interest of your business in the long run.

A common mistake made by several taxpayers is that they never keep themselves updated with the recent developments in taxation laws. Taxes are not fixed, and they tend to change from one year to another. Also, taxes vary from one state to another. The taxes applicable also change depending on the political climate. If you don't stay updated on recent taxation trends, then your business might not be able to make the most of the new tax breaks available.

If you don't maintain the records or if you have outsourced the filing of taxes to someone else, ensure that you disclose everything to the CPA. If you don't provide the CPA or the accountant with all the details they need, they will not be able to provide true and fair tax records.

If your tax records are not maintained properly, it can spell trouble for your business. Apart from this, if the accounts are fabricated, then even the business owners can be held personally liable for fraudulent practices. Also, if you don't disclose the necessary information to the CPA or other professionals, they will not be able to do their job properly. After all, how can they suggest the best deductions and tax credits available, if they don't have any information about your small business?

Common Business Tax Mistakes

Although some aspects of the tax system are dreadfully and unnecessarily complex, no law says you can't benefit from the pitfalls of others. This can save you from unnecessary expenses in the future, and with this objective in mind, this section outlines familiar tax goof-ups made by small business owners when it relates to making business decisions, tax deductions, and managing income.

Many of these are costly tax-related mistakes that you have to watch out for, not just for optimal tax management but also to manage your business finances in the best way. Many of these are quite subtle, and here lies the danger – the costly danger.

Trusting Your Bookkeeper Too Much

I'm not saying it's a mistake to trust your bookkeeper – of course, it isn't! However, there's such a thing as too much of a good thing can become bad. And when it comes to your bookkeeper, that holds true.

To this extent, you shouldn't trust your bookkeeper with cash-handling functions. If you give your bookkeeper the ability and authority to disburse cash and record transactions in the books, you're practically giving him or her the license to embezzle funds from your business, including money that's supposed to be paid to the government for taxes. More than just under filing your business's taxes, which is in and by itself already a costly mistake, you also run the risk of bleeding your business dry to the point of paying no more taxes, i.e., closed down.

Make sure that your bookkeeper's function is limited to keeping his or her hands on the business's accounting books – no more and no less. Assign a person with no access to the business's books to handle cash-related functions to prevent theft and embezzlement.

Failure to Submit the Required Taxes

You need to provide projected periodic tax obligations when expected, whether you are self-employed, or you receive a substantial amount of taxable income from investments beyond retirement accounts. As a business owner, you must also deduct taxes for your workers and submit these taxes to the relevant tax authorities. Many owners of smallholdings or companies do not have a department whose particular duties are to deduct taxes; hence, they drive themselves into a persistent tax trap by refusing to make calculated periodic tax payments. Well, it's not a crime yet, you can plan that tax payment and save yourself from unnecessary penalties in the future.

Using Your Financial and Tax Consultants the Wrong Way

Sometimes relying on your knowledge and that of IRS publications for tax-related issues is not to be recommended, specifically for business owners with tax trouble.

Most people find the IRS guidelines boring and, in fact, far from the main deal, which is to reduce their tax fees. Some parts of this book can guide you through the process. If the uncertainty of your small business and tax decisions begins to overwhelm you, you can seek the help of your tax and financial consultants.

Assessing and evaluating your skill as a small business owner can go a long way as well. You can decide to appraise your accountability and operational expertise. This will help to detect when and when not to bring in a tax or a financial consultant.

Remember that when you face multiple tax long term issues, using a tax professional will be worthwhile. If your tax condition remains difficult or if you know you'd be doing an even worse job on your own, use a tax professional instead. Try recruiting and paying a professional to sort out your taxes once if your condition is unchanging or not that difficult. You can go ahead and try to complete your tax returns yourself after that.

Looking for Quick Help After a Significant Business Decision

Many people seek information and hire help after making a decision, even though it is usually smarter financial-wise to seek the advice of a qualified professional regarding a business decision; it is more efficient to seek proactive help ahead of time.

Educate yourself before making that big business and financial decisions for your small business. The good thing is that you are already a step ahead, as this book can help give more reasonable insights regarding any questions you may have.

Too Much Tax Buffer

Often, people are ecstatic when they or their businesses receive a large amount as a tax refund, which is the result of setting aside too much money for withholding taxes. Better to overpay than underpay taxes, right? Right and wrong!

That's right because certainly, anything other than underpayment of taxes is the better option. Wrong because just because it's better than under-declaring and paying your taxes doesn't mean it's the best thing to do. Regularly paying too much in taxes – as indicated by regularly receiving large tax refunds – means you're giving the government free money for a significant amount of time. It's free because you don't get paid interest for lending the excess money to the government.

The best thing to do is prepare your taxes well to the point that refunds – if any – are minimal. You're better off using the excess money for more productive uses like investments or increasing inventory in anticipation of bigger sales.

Not Maintaining A Tax Organizer

It will be in your best interest to maintain a tax organizer – and an accurate one at that. Why? It's because a tax organizer can help you make your tax records pretty much invincible to IRS scrutiny. They do this by providing you with all the possible questions that the IRS may require you to answer concerning specific types of expenses that you deduct from your taxable income, such as entertainment, travel, and others like it. Further, having a tax organizer enables you to shift the burden of proof to the IRS auditors who may be tasked to audit your business, should that happen. Not maintaining a tax organizer is a costly mistake as it increases the chances of the IRS auditors finding "loopholes" in your tax declarations, which can subject you to certain costly penalties or sanctions.

Hiring A Tax Professional When You Can Do It Yourself

Hiring a tax professional will cost you money. There are instances when doing your business taxes yourself is ideal because it can save you good money in the long run – money that you can use to grow your business instead. But if you hire someone to do something that you can easily do well yourself for your own business, this will lead to unnecessary expenses.

Doing Your Business Taxes Yourself

While hiring a tax professional can be costly, it can save you more money in the long run by ensuring you're able to report and pay the right amount of taxes on your business's operations regularly and on time. If you choose to do it yourself and you're not equipped enough for the task, you'll eventually spend more money on penalties and charges when the IRS finds that you understated or paid your business's taxes late.

The following are some of the common mistakes which small business owners make because they don't hire tax consultants.

Mixing Personal and Business Finances

Small businesses such as Schedule C entities mostly make one of the biggest mistakes known as the "comingling" of personal and business accounts. That said, having different credit and bank accounts isn't something you should strictly follow. Most tax professionals recommend having separate accounts because this ensures accurate financial reporting as well as bookkeeping; this also makes your taxes much more manageable.

When business owners maintain a precise balance sheet, many expenses become more easily identifiable. The same applies to advantages related to tax when you have separate finances; income and expenses become easy to identify. In case of a mixed account, there is an increased chance that you might miss deductible business expenses, or you might be left with some unreported income.

Misclassifying Independent Contractors and Employees

Some small business owners might think that there is no significant difference between an independent contractor and an employee, but this is not the case. The IRS has released a complete document regarding the differences between an employee and an independent contractor (self-employed). The gist of the document is mentioned in the following key points:

Does the business supply for tools and other stuff without applying any additional costs to the person, or the business gets refunded for the expenses?

Does the business decide the working hours, and does it choose when, where, and how the person works on their given task?

Is the working relationship thought of as a continuous and essential aspect of the whole business, and are there any defined benefits or contracts such as insurance, pension, and vacation time?

Misclassifying a person as an independent contractor who should have been considered as an employee can result in penalties and interest because the owner might not have paid the shares of the taxes related to employment. Businesses should also make sure that they have given a Form 1099-Misc to contractors who have been paid more than $600, and a Form W-2 has also been given to every employee.

If you didn't pay the employer share, also known as the self-employment taxes for an independent contractor, you and the self-employed individual might get in a difficult situation with the IRS. The self-employment taxes should be included with the estimated quarterly tax payments, to avoid any unwanted situations from arising,

Missing Out on Valid Deductions or Overstating Business

If some of your expenses are outside the standard percentage thresholds, or over several years, you have some expenses which exceed the income of your business; you will quickly get the attention of the IRS. The computers at IRS are consistently comparing your expenses like meals, entertainment, business travel, printing supplies, and other legitimate deductions against the same kinds of costs of other similar small businesses.

In Schedule C small businesses, many items are used for both personal and commercial purposes. Expenses related to these mixed-used assets often put these small businesses in challenging situations. The IRS has strict rules regarding the home office uses. If a room is specified for business, it shouldn't be used for any other purpose. And if you use part of your house exclusively for a business, you might be eligible for the "home office deduction." According to the IRS, your home must meet two basic requirements to qualify as a deduction. First, part of the house should be regularly and exclusively used for business, and second, you must prove that your home is used as your principal place of business. There are many other deductible expenses that IRS defines as "necessary and ordinary" part of running a business– just make sure that you don't misplace any receipts. Still, many Schedule C filers miss the opportunity of obtaining these deductions when preparing their taxes. This thing usually happens to those who mix their personal and business accounts. There is an online resource center of the IRS, which can be used to determine how a specific business expense should be handled. During the year, a small business has been established, there are many operating expenses which are considered as deductible. Although, over several years, capital expenses like the cost of manufacturing equipment, buildings, and purchasing vehicles, etc., can become devalued.

Not Paying Enough to the Shareholders of the S-Corporation

For the businesses recognized as an S-Corp, the IRS recommends that appropriate wages should be paid to the shareholders of the company; the amount of the payments should be enough so that it can be considered as taxable income. These wages should be given out before the non-wage distributions are made because taxes are applied differently on the non-wage distributions.

The Form 1120S, U.S. income tax return, is a tax document used for an S Corporation to report financial matters of S-Corp's shareholders. The official instructions for this document state that S corporation's different payments and distributions provided to the shareholder (corporate officer) should be considered as wages, and the amount of the salary should be reasonable enough that it compensates the services of the shareholder. In simple terms, it means that if the corporate officer takes part in day-to-day activities of the management and operations of the business, that person should be considered as an employee and should be paid according to the work he/she is doing.

Frequently Asked Questions

Here are the questions most frequently asked of the IRS about filing taxes.

• Question: How do I let the IRS know of my recent address change? Answer: You can do one of the following: file Form 8822 to change your address, use your new address when you file a tax return, send the IRS a written and signed statement with your name, old address, new address, and SSN, ITIN, or EIN, or notify the IRS via telephone or in-person.

• Question: When must I stop claiming my child as my dependent? Answer: You can no longer claim your child as your dependent when he or she no longer meets the qualifying child test. To pass the qualifying child test, your child must be a student younger than 24 years of age or younger than 19 years of age by the end of the calendar year. If your child is "permanently and totally disabled," your child permanently meets the qualifying child test, and you can keep claiming your child as your dependent without limit.

• Question: What is the maximum income that can be earned by a single dependent student before he or she is required to file an income tax return? Answer: Use Publication 501 to determine if you need to file an income tax return.

• Question: If I made an error on my tax return and filed it, what should I do? Answer: Mathematical errors are often caught and corrected by the IRS in the processing of the return. If your error involved incorrect income, deductions, or credits or the wrong filing status, file an amended return using Form 1040X.

Chapter 11: 3 Secrets Tips to Reduce Taxes Legally for LLC & Sole Proprietorship

One of the things you can know to ask is if you need to get help from a professional to handle your corporate tax — and help you plan so you can take advantage of certain deductions. "I'm also asked how to decide when to talk to a professional, and there are two ways to get it done," says Colombik. "Another way is to look at the tax and decide if talking to a lawyer will cost me less than paying my tax bill. Another way is to think that if you're not paying a lot of tax in that area right now, but you know you're going to be in the future, you should figure out if there's a way to plan properly."

Here are just a few examples:

• Contribute to a pension plan. If your company is successful, You will exclude income from a covered pension plan, which will allow you a tax deduction for your assets, delay tax on contributions earnings (in the end, tax is paid when you start to make money from the program, usually at retirement). And, if you have employees, you can earn employee loyalty to provide them with an opportunity to save on retirement. Learn more about the retirement plan choices from IRS Publication 560, Small Business Retreat Plans, at www.irs.gov. You give up a 401(k) share, as a small business owner. Although several retirement account choices optimize retirement savings and reap significant tax benefits, you can miss the free money available through the match. For example, the IRS allows you to put away up to $53,000 of retirement, with the Individual 401(k).

Result: The reimbursement shall not be included in the W-2 form of the workers (the employees are not paid on the reimbursements), and on these sums the company avoids payroll taxes (FICA and unemployment taxes) Read more about accounting plans at www.irs.gov in IRS Publication 463, Travel, Entertainment, Gifts, and Car Expenses.

• Defer taxes and expedite deductions. You may take several measures to move taxes into the next tax year by the end of the year and raise your deductions in the current tax year. "Take your bills out a few days later over the last month of the year," Colombik says. This means getting paid in January of the next year a few days later and being able to defer the salary, rather than being paid in December of the current year and having to report this income immediately. Likewise, another way of speeding deductions is to see what expenses you owe in January and to pay them before the end of December, so that you can take the deduction in the current year.

• Correctly structure your business. This is the "single most overlooked aspect of tax planning." Most small start-ups don't change their business structure when they ought. For instance, if you have a closely-held business in which you, the owner, earn the profits, they are usually set up as an LLC or an S. While there is nothing wrong with these structures, you may be able to gain tax benefits by structuring your company as a C corporation where the first $50,000 of your income is taxed at a rate of 15 percent compared to a rate of 35 percent if you are in the highest tax bracket.

• Consider adding incentives rather than promotions to employee benefits. Another way to save taxes for you and your employees is to pay them by your contribution to their health insurance costs, rather than charging them the same amount in terms of wage increases.

Employ a family member. One of the best ways for your small business to cut taxes is by hiring a family member. Internal Revenue Service (IRS) provides for a variety of options, all with the potential benefit of tax revenue protection. You can even hire your kids, who are as young as seven.

The profit isn't going to stop hiring your kids. Sometimes, the IRS lets you employ a partner. You may be able to set aside pension savings for them, thus reducing the taxable liability, depending on the benefits they get through another career.

Raise Money for Healthcare Needs: By putting aside money for healthcare needs, one of the easiest ways to reduce small business taxes is. If you have a highly deductible health plan which qualifies, you can do this through a Health Savings Account (HSA). It is also encouraged that every business owner consider the use of HSA. When medical costs are increasing, more companies are looking to lower the health insurance costs. Business and workers will reduce taxes and potentially related medical costs by using HSAs.

Switch company arrangement: You don't have the option of an employer paying a percentage of your taxes as a small business owner. You're in the dark for all the Social Security and Medicare payments. These sums only lift an already high tax bill. You still have to pay those taxes if your company is taxed as a Limited Liability Company (LLC).

In some cases, you will remove one of those two tax liabilities from the employer. In this transition, there are many things to consider, such as paying yourself a reasonable salary and other associated risks. Still, it can be an excellent way to reduce your taxable liability. Deduct travel expenses If you are traveling a lot for work as well as fun, you may be able to reduce your business taxes. Business travel is entirely deductible, although the same advantage does not extend to personal travel. There are several ways to save on business taxes to manage travel. Personal travel may be paired with a justifiable business purpose. You can also benefit from the frequent flier miles you earn on your travel.

Hire Independent Contractors: You won't need to withhold federal or state income taxes from their earnings by hiring independent contractors. And, you won't have to pay the employer share of taxes on Social Security and Medicare or provide unemployment benefits. Also, make sure the contractor isn't deemed an employee by the IRS, or you'll have to pay back taxes and fines. Have a tax professional seek advice before classifying someone as an independent contractor.

Maximize Deductions: Two ways to maximize deductions are to keep outstanding records and receipts and to rely on advice from a tax professional.

Pay Your Bills by Year's End: If your business-related bills (rent, telephone, power, etc.) are due in early January but cover the previous year's expenses, take out the checkbook before New Year's start. All of these expenses can help to mid-April reduce your tax burden.

Once you upgrade your old computer or subscribe to this awesome new business newsletter, you may be waiting for a tad more revenue to flow in. Yet tax-wise, investing in your company now is wiser, rather than waiting for the New Year. In particular, lousy equipment can cause headaches for small businesses: support yourself by repairing or replacing worn-out goods next week and get some of that investment back into deductions that could give you money back next year.

Give Charity: The old computer you've just replaced could support a non-profit organization. They can't afford new equipment while reducing the tax burden on your small business. The IRS offers tax incentives for contributions, so make the most of them. Review to ensure the charity is eligible, and the contributions are tax-deductible before donating. The IRS also specifies that you have written the organization's acknowledgment for donations of up to or valued at $250.

Use the Welfare-to-Work Tax Credit: The Work Opportunity Tax Credit (WOTC) program, which provides the federal tax credit' Welfare-to-Work,' is an opportunity designed to encourage the hiring of individuals from specific communities with a disproportionately high unemployment rate or other special job needs, such as veterans, ex-felons and at-risk young people. Organizations eligible to take part in the WOTC system will minimize their federal tax liability by up to $2,400 per recruit. The Welfare-to-Work tax credit provides an incentive for employers to help individuals transition from welfare to work. For each eligible new employee, companies that hire under this WOTC category will minimize their federal tax liability by up to $9,000 over two years.

Conclusion

Taxes have been around since the dawn of civilization. There is a popular quote by Benjamin Franklin that says, "There are only two things certain in life - death and taxes." Therefore, it wouldn't be wise to overlook the importance of taxes. There are several types of taxes and not just the income tax that taxpayers have to pay.

As with individuals, even businesses are treated as separate entities when it comes to taxes. The way an individual pays taxes, small businesses are considered to be artificial personas for the sake of taxation. So, a small business has several tax obligations.

Unless you are aware of the different tax obligations, the rate of taxation, and how to file taxes, you cannot run a successful business. Also, to avoid any unnecessary penalties and fines, the business must always pay its taxes on time. So, there are various things you must learn about if you want to successfully understand taxes in comprehensive detail.

Now that you have reached the end of this book, the idea of taxes probably doesn't seem as overwhelming as it once did. For the sake of your business's health and bottom-line, it is important to always take care of your taxes. If you want a stress-free tax season and learn to save money while you pay all your taxes, then this is the perfect book for you. Irrespective of whether it's a small or a major business decision, everything has a tax consequence. From deduction of certain expenses to tax write-offs, and the business model you follow are some of the different things you must take into consideration.

In this book, you were given all the information you will need to understand the basics of taxes. This book is a simple and comprehensive guide filled with easy to understand and practical tips about taxes. It helps you understand all your rights and obligations while you navigate the world of taxes.

Once you're armed with all the information given in this book, you can easily save time and money required to do taxes. Also, it empowers you to prepare and understand all the important tax documents associated with a small business. Regardless of whether you decide to hire external help for taxes or not, you will always have the information required to get things done by yourself.

So, now all that's left for you to do is use the information given in this book. You don't have to implement all the practices at once. Instead, choose the practices that are well suited for your business and requirements and implement them immediately. As with any other aspect of your life, it takes plenty of patience, effort, and consistency to truly understand the vast area of taxation. However, once you get the hang of it, you will finally realize how simple taxes are. It is not rocket science, and there is nothing to worry about if you don't understand it as soon as you try your hand at it the first time. You will get there with practice and better understanding. It is now time to take control of your business, taxes, and all other financial accounts today.

Credit Secrets

7 Strategies to Raise your Credit Score Fast, Repair your Negative Profile and Get Out of Debt to Finally Change Your Financial Life

[Lucas Anderson]

Legal & Disclaimer

The information contained in this book and its contents is not designed to replace or take the place of any form of medical or professional advice; and is not meant to replace the need for independent medical, financial, legal or other professional advice or services, as may be required. The content and information in this book has been provided for educational and entertainment purposes only.

The content and information contained in this book has been compiled from sources deemed reliable, and it is accurate to the best of the Author's knowledge, information and belief. However, the Author cannot guarantee its accuracy and validity and cannot be held liable for any errors and/or omissions. Further, changes are periodically made to this book as and when needed. Where appropriate and/or necessary, you must consult a professional (including but not limited to your doctor, attorney, financial advisor or such other professional advisor) before using any of the suggested remedies, techniques, or information in this book.

Upon using the contents and information contained in this book, you agree to hold harmless the Author from and against any damages, costs, and expenses, including any legal fees potentially resulting from the application of any of the information provided by this book. This disclaimer applies to any loss, damages or injury caused by the use and application, whether directly or indirectly, of any advice or information presented, whether for breach of contract, tort, negligence, personal injury, criminal intent, or under any other cause of action.

You agree to accept all risks of using the information presented inside this book.

You agree that by continuing to read this book, where appropriate and/or necessary, you shall consult a professional (including but not limited to your doctor, attorney, or financial advisor or such other advisor as needed) before using any of the suggested remedies, techniques, or information in this book.

Table of Contents

Introduction

A good credit score plays a vital role in helping you maintain your financial condition. Most Americans do not understand what a credit score is all about. It's now evident that a lot of Americans are yet to know the importance of maintaining or improving their credit score even if they are not hoping to apply for the loan in the future. The important thing here is that regardless of whether you take a loan or mortgage now or in the future, it is necessary to have a good credit report. Not having this can deny you access to make big purchases such as cars and houses because oftentimes, your loan's interest rate is determined by your credit score. A really low or bad score does not only affect your rates but can lead you into serious trouble if not immediately addressed.

It is better to have a good credit score at the beginning and maintain it than to have a bad score and try fixing it because to fix your credit score; it is a function of who you give to help you fix and also the information you open yourself to. Because depending on if you spend thousands of dollars to have it fixed or go-ahead to fix it by yourself, you might hurt your credit report even more, hence causing more harm than good.

Chapter 1: The Importance of Good Credit Score

Obtaining the valuable credit score goes a long way to make a choice on if the funds should be loaned or not. This also helps these entities that want to extend credits to know the precise amount of money to give the person as well as with what interest rate.

Experian, Equifax, and TransUnion are the three most common credit reporting agencies. Each of these companies offers a free credit report individually, making it a total of three reports per year. From this, you can tell that it is necessary that one reads and understands the contents that are on the report. Information such as errors in the amount of money to be paid back, payment histories and errors in late payment content can be seen. It also helps to confirm that there is no identity theft in the report.

Companies offering credit will be cautious in taking a closer look at numbers on the credit score of an individual. Lenders believe that a score of 700 or above is a very excellent one. One should value keeping their scores high at all times because there seem to be several advantages of obtaining a high credit score. Credit extensions having low-interest rate offers would definitely be secured by the high scoring report owners. Moreover, for those with high credit scores, credit approval processes are normally done super-fast (in little or no time).

Before applying for a big loan, it is important to note that the one who wants to credit is expected to screen their report at least up to six to twelve months approximately. Checking the score helps you see for yourself that the details are listed correctly and fish out errors that may not seem to tally. In a case where there are errors, the period earlier mentioned allows the one seeking credit to properly address the errors that may have occurred. In a case where errors on the report still surface at the time of applying for a large loan, it is still critical that the lender is made aware of these mistakes depending on the situation.

Just as this book teaches, it is possible to improve your credit score. One of the ways this can be done is ensuring you pay all owed money on a regular basis hence reducing your outstanding account balances. Since deadlines of payments are noted on every report, it is always best to pay in good time. For the borrower's sake, it would be advisable not to take on new debt.

To round this up, here are a few things I'll mention that point you to receiving a good credit score:

Speaking with creditors and credit advisors will be a major advantage for you as there are cases where one might be faced with a really terrible financial crisis where payments cannot be made within that time. The creditors would most likely be ready to assist to the best of their ability, especially when it comes to lowering and spreading out payments.

Do not allow your credit card balances go to the roofs. Making them as low as possible is vital. I do not advise you to let them go high.

One thing that makes me laugh about some people is that they think they can improve their credit score by simply just closing their old accounts, so they hide late payments displayed on those accounts. It doesn't work that way. The late payment history will still show on the credit report, even if that account is closed.

Lenders always check to see the credit history with active borrowing of previous years or more.

Achieving a good credit score range might not be easy at first, but it will go a long way to boost your personal financial life. All this must be done with a sense of keen insight as well as careful thinking.

Chapter 2: How Credit Score is Calculated

The credit score is calculated using several pieces of your credit report. If you want to have a high credit score or have good credit, you must know how it is calculated and what factors (banks and credit agencies) to take into account to approve or deny a loan or credit card. Your credit score is calculated based on these categories, namely:

· The amounts that you owe

· The history of Payment

· What types of open accounts you have

· The age of the accounts

· The number of credit applications

Let's examine these factors and see how we can raise your credit score one by one.

1. The amounts that you owe

It is no coincidence that the amounts that you owe is the next thing to discuss. This is because, after the history of payment, it is known to be the next most influencing factor of your credit score.

It is already a general rule that you are required to use only 30% of the credit the bank approves to you and nothing more than that. It will be highly unwise if you go ahead to use all the credit that the bank approves, say $300 on a $1000 credit card. That means you should never make use of the maximum account that has been allowed on your card. Credit bureaus perceive this as an omen when you start to depend on the money and they tend to withdraw as it signifies a negative mark for your credit report and also your credit score.

I would advise you to use below 30% of your credit, or what's best is you could go-ahead to use only 10% of your credit line and nothing more than that. By doing this, you will have better credit scores and your chances of increasing and even sustaining a good credit score will be limitless.

The amount of money that you owe is also a key factor to consider when calculating your score.

2.   The history of payment

Consider making payments on or even earlier than the agreed time as it is absolutely important and has a major impact on your score. If you are one that makes late payments, then your credit score will dramatically reduce.

The fundamental thing a lender would want to find out is whether or not you paid your bills or even your credit loans in a good time. This category out of the others majorly influences your credit score and makes up to 35% of your score, which is why it is very important to take note of it.

Now that you know that delayed payments can affect your credit score and also hinder you from building a good credit history, you must do well to ensure you pay all debts on time without any qualms.

The types of accounts normally considered for payment history are namely:

·   Installment Loans
·   Credit Cards (such as Visa, Master Card and so on)
·   Loans to the consumer
·   Retail accounts and;
·   Mortgage Loans

Remember, the path of making and building a good credit score is a path that will require you to make payments on time.

3. What types of open accounts you have

Another factor that can favor your credit score is having various types of loans (mortgages, cars, and student loans) and credit cards.

Your credit score is majorly concerned with the different types of credit that you use, some of which exist are credit cards, mortgage loans, installment loans and accounts with finance companies too.

Do take note that it is not so important that you use each one of them and I'll advise that you only open accounts that you really are going to use.

The credit mix has no major effect on your credit score, but it is of great importance that your credit report does not contain excess information on which your score is based.

As it were, there is really no perfect version of a credit mix as it varies with time from individual to individual. Opening car loans, student loans and credit cards you won't be needing won't be advisable for you. Although, it would be an added advantage to have this factor that shows that you know how to handle your credit responsibly.

4. The age of the accounts

Consistency is key in the credit score world. As long as you keep maintaining a good credit score history, your credit score will always remain high. The general rule explains it as the longer you have credit cards, the more your credit score increases. That's why I'll advise you to start your credit as soon as you can. This is a factor that constitutes about 15% of your credit score, measuring the length at which you have your credit accounts and how well you have been able to manage them within that period.

Here are what your FICO credit score records:

· It takes into account the age of both the new and old accounts and even an average age of all of your accounts.

· It also takes into account your credit lines (if you have), how long you have been with them and how your payment history has been.

·   And finally, it measures the exact age of your loans/credit cards. Because of this, many professionals advise that older accounts should neither be closed nor canceled as it is likely to affect your credit score. There's a high possibility of you having a high credit score by having a long time with your credit.

5.   The number of credit applications

Lastly, the number of applications to your credit slightly affects your credit score. Every time you apply for a loan or possibly a credit card (even if not yet approved), your credit score slightly decreases.

Opening various credit accounts within a very short time can be very risky for financial institutions, most especially when it's a case of one who does not have a lengthy credit history. This explains why many people see that their credit score has decreased either when they open a credit card or approved for a particular loan. However, the decline is temporary.

Also, bear in mind that credit checks vary. Interestingly, checking your credit will have your credit score reduced if and only if it is a hard inquiry. There are hard inquiry and soft inquiry of which I will explain below.

The hard inquiry is made when a loan is applied with a lender. That may include a student loan, car, mortgage loan. These inquiries affect your credit score.

While the soft inquiry is made when you request a copy of your credit report, apply for a job or maybe use it for a credit monitoring service. These types of inquiries in no way affect your credit score.

How exactly is it calculated?

As important as it is to calculate your credit score, it is also very important to know that these factors have no fixed percentage as they may vary due to the financial information obtained from your credit report.

This goes to say that without adequate knowledge of the basic factors above, there is a tendency for an individual to be careless in the decisions he makes at obtaining a high credit score. It is hence very important that these factors are known.

Though these factors are applied when calculating a credit report, the level of importance varies from person to person.

It is not possible to record the impact of each of the factors on the credit score without acknowledging the report as a whole.

How to check your credit score

Some services enable you to check your credit score at very little or no cost. However, you must take caution and use services that you know are reliable, so you don't fall into the hands of scammers on the Internet. Some of these reliable services, especially the ones listed below, have no cost.

Some of these services are:

Experian: - This US credit agency is used by several lenders to evaluate your credit and requires you to pay just $1 to view your credit.

TransUnion: - This credit bureau also allows you to see your score quickly and easily. It is also used lenders as well as banks to estimate your credit.

Quizzle: - This is a credit score simulator that offers a Vantage Score that is based on TransUnion data.

Mint.com: - This is another simulator that utilizes data from the Equifax credit agency.

Credit cards that allow you to see your credit score

It is also very possible to obtain your credit score for FREE by having some particular credit cards at your disposal. Asides the bonus rewards you get, these cards improve the quality of your credit score and notify you immediately there is any form of suspicious activity. Here are two that I can guarantee are simply the best.

Discover IT credit card

Discover IT credit card is known to be one of the best credit cards of recent. This card uses Experian data to display your credit score monthly.

Monthly, your credit tracker is updated, notifying you of sudden changes in your credit report. Also, it is accepted internationally and is relatively easy to obtain.

CreditWise from Capital One

The Capital One credit cards feature the CreditWise credit simulator, which uses TransUnion data to give you a weekly evaluation of your credit score.

It allows you to predict and calculate a cause-and-effect situation if you paid all debts or made payments on time for either 6 or 12 months and so on.

It is available to Capital One bank customers using any of their credit cards.

Chapter 3: The Right Way to Check your Credit Report

The business uses the credit and pays the bill promptly. As the business has established a positive business credit profile, and as the business continues using the credit and paying the bills on time, it will qualify for more credit.

The first step in business credit building is for the business owner to order a credit report for the business. It is very important for the business owner to know what really is being reported for that business in regard both to positive and derogatory information. The business owner will also want to actively monitor the business credit building and score building as it is taking place.

Business Credit Reports

Many business owners find, when they receive their Business Information Report from D&B, that they have a low PAYDEX score. They scratch their heads and wonder why their score is low even when they are paying the bills on time.

A business owner cannot find out which companies are reporting negative information to your file without having a credit report. However, a business owner can obtain a list of all the companies that are reporting to the business credit file. Upon request, the business owner will get an alphabetical list of all the companies reporting to the business credit bureau as well as the number of times they reported.

On page 2 of the report will be an overview of the companies that have reported and the dollar-weighted payments. The Paydex score will also be on the report. Each of the companies listed will be sorted by supplier industry. If there are less than 20 companies on the list, the D&B

representative might choose to simply read the list over the phone or e-mail the information to the business owner.

Other information on this report includes the total dollar amount of all trades reported, the largest amount that anyone trade has reported, and the percentage of payments that have been made to the top ten (10) industries.

The Experian Smart Business credit report will tell the business owner how many trade lines are reporting and show if a business credit score has been assigned if the business has an active Experian Business Profile, and if the business has had any recent credit inquiries.

Once a business sets up its credit report and pays some bills on time, it should have a high PAYDEX score. It is then vital that the business maintain its report.

The business owner should check the business report periodically. They may want to consider purchasing the Monitoring Service that D&B offers. This service allows a business to receive alerts when new positive or negative information appears on the report. There are several areas that a business owner will be notified of if they change including:

☐ Credit Rating

☐ Suits, liens or business judgments

☐ PAYDEX score changes

☐ Changes to financial statements

☐ Other significant business news

It is extremely important that the business credit file remain accurate. The Fair Credit Reporting Act does not apply to businesses as it does with consumer reports. If there is something wrong on the business credit report, or if a step is skipped in setting it up, there is no legal recourse to have that information removed. If the file was set up incorrectly, there's a good chance the business credit file could be put in the "High Risk" category, making it nearly impossible to remove inaccuracies.

This is your Credit Scorecard as of 05/20/2016. Come back after 30 days to refresh it.

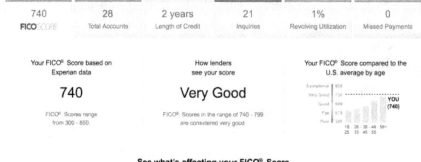

740	28	2 years	21	1%	0
FICO SCORE	Total Accounts	Length of Credit	Inquiries	Revolving Utilization	Missed Payments

Your FICO® Score based on Experian data	How lenders see your score	Your FICO® Score compared to the U.S. average by age
740	**Very Good**	YOU (740)
FICO® Scores range from 300 - 850.	FICO® Scores in the range of 740 - 799 are considered very good	

See what's affecting your FICO® Score

↑ What's helping   ↓ What's hurting

Chapter 4: How to Repair Your Negative Profile

Where to Start Repairing Your Credit

If you realize that your score is low, there are certain drastic measures you need to take in order to address the situation.

-Stop using credit cards. If your circumstances demand that you must use a credit card at some point, use the credit cards with the lowest interest rate. Cheap is the catch phrase for you now because you are trying to resolve a credit score crisis. It has a lot to do with your spending habits.

-Deposit as much as you can to the cards that charge the highest interest. Just meet the minimum for the other cards in the meantime. This is one of debt recovery strategies. It is more like an inverted snowball approach.

-Don't open new credit accounts as you are trying to repair your damaged credit score rating. Don't jump from one problem to the next. New credit accounts will simply lead you down the same road of destruction as has happened in the current situation.

-Avoid opening new credit accounts in a short span of time. This often happens when you are looking for funding for college. Although some agencies have a waiver for such enquires if they are done within a span of a month, others still consider such applications and factor them in your credit report. You are therefore advised to spend a much shorter time shopping for funding for your college fees. The exceptions notwithstanding, such acts are generalized considered an indication of poor financial management.

Let's take a look at the strategies you can use to repair your credit.

Identify theft claim

Over 16 million Americans are victims of identity theft. This is definitely a large population so anyone could be a victim. Identity theft is a crime, which involves the police so ensure you are ready to go this route. If you are sure that your score has been ruined because of identity theft, you can use this method. Abusing this method could land you into trouble with the law. Here is how to dispute using the method:

Step 1: Report the matter to the police then get a copy of your report from the local sheriff (you will need this report later)

Step2: File the dispute with FTC using this link **here**.

Step 3: Go on to dispute with various credit bureaus.

Step4: Set up an identity theft alert (be sure to know what this means in terms of your access to credit).

Pay the original creditor

You don't want multiple collection agencies reporting new items every month since this hurts your score. Simply send a check with full payment of the outstanding amount to the original creditor then send proof of the payment to the collection agencies that have reported that debt. After that, you then request that they should delete all the derogatory items from your credit report. You can blend this with the pay to delete strategy mentioned above.

Pay to delete

In this strategy, you agree to pay a creditor only if they agree to delete such items from the credit report. I mentioned about zero balances; don't fall for the trap of creditors who say they will mark it as zero. Zero is not good for you because it shows you have been having problems in the past (this sticks in your credit report for 7 or more years)! In simple terms, your report shouldn't be showing that you have had a bad credit history with derogatory items. If the creditor is interested in their money more than tainting your credit, they will agree to this. If the information passes to collection agencies after 2 years, you can also use this strategy to make them stop reporting your settled debt; in any case, they buy the debts for a tiny fraction so anything they get will probably be good enough! This is the best time (when the debt is with the collection agencies) to use the pay to delete strategy because you have more bargaining power. If the collection agency doesn't accept your offer, its only option is through a judgment.

Note#1: Use pay to delete when you start noticing new derogative items in your report since these could easily hurt your credit. You might even start seeing multiple collection companies reporting the same debt. In such times, you have an advantage since you negotiate everything on your terms; if one does not accept your offer, another will definitely take it.

Note#2: Have everything put in writing if they agree on your terms. If they cannot put it in writing, don't pay. After paying, you should give it about 45 days to reflect in your credit report. Don't take anything less than deletion; don't accept updating balance. If they cannot delete, don't pay. The process is pretty fast so they shouldn't give you excuses that they cannot delete; mention the Universal Data Form to make them know that you know that it is possible.

Note#3: Choose your battles well i.e. Don't use this strategy on creditors who have a lot to lose because they might sue you to compel you to pay. Aim for creditors who have already been barred by statute of limitation (2 years have passed), which means they cannot sue you in court to compel you to pay.

Settle your debt

Total debt owed accounts for up to 30% of the credit score so don't overlook this. This includes personal loans, car loan, and credit utilization. You should also calculate the credit utilization ratio (the balance you carry in your revolving fund compared to your credit). As your credit utilization increases, your credit score goes down; aim to keep your credit card balances no more than 30% of your credit card limit. You should even aim for zero balances since this means higher credit score. Combine this strategy with pay to delete strategy.

To pay your debts, you can use the snowballing or avalanching strategies. Snowballing involves paying off debts with the lowest balance first then closing them as you move up to the bigger debts. Avalanching involves paying debts starting from those with the highest interest rates as you move down.

Lookout for errors in the report

I mentioned that 93% of the credit reports have been proven to have errors. Look out for any of these then file a dispute. Such things like last date of activity, write off date, wrong account name or number and others could be enough to taint your credit. Don't overlook any of that. If the report really has an error, don't be discouraged by the credit bureau's stalling tactics; mention the Notice (Summons) and complaint to make them know that you are really aware of what the law requires of them. The bureaus wouldn't want to have their systems investigated and proven to be weak/flawed so this strategy can actually compel them to correct errors thus boosting your credit.

Mix/spread your credit

This usually affects your credit score by up to 10%. Having more types of credit signifies that you can handle your finances properly making you credit worthy especially if you have a good payment history.

Request for proof of the original debt

If you are sure that the credit card has been written off due to late payment, there are times when the carriers might not have the original billing statements within 30days as stipulated by the law. With this, you can get the item removed from your report such that it appears as if the entry was not even there. You can also request for the original contract that you actually signed when applying for a credit card. You shouldn't just ask for verification because by doing so, you ask the collection agency to verify that they received your request for collection on an account that bears your name. You should be clear on what you want them to do; in this case, they should provide proof of debt including giving you statements for the last few months and the original contract, which you signed.

Handy tips to improve your score

*Avoid Bad Signals

One of the subtle indications that your report may pick and affect you negatively includes using your credit card to a pawnshop. Although it is not an objective assessment of your financial situation, the readership will develop qualms about you. Such actions speak volumes about your financial organization ability.

*Do Not Delete Your Past Good Debt Records

Your credit history speaks volumes about your consistency. This is the information the lender looks for to decide whether you are a good or bad risk.

*Use fewer cards

The small nuisance balances on your cards adversely affect your score. Many people do not realize that it is more expensive to use more credit cards. It is even harder to manage them. Consequently, the chance of defaulting or making a late payment is significantly increased when you use several cards.

*Minimize the lowest interest rate loan hunt period

When you apply for many loans within a short period, the credit report often reflects several loans instead of the final one you might have settled on a month later.

*Get a settlement letter when you settle any debt then send the letter to the different bureaus to have any derogatory items removed.

Settle your bills promptly

Payment history accounts for 35% of your credit score making it one of the biggest determinants of the score. This is pretty straight forward; when you pay your bills on time, your score will improve. You could even set up automatic payments just to ensure that you won't miss payments since the amounts are deducted from your account. The biggest contributors to this include collections, bankruptcies, and different late payments. You should not that the recent delinquencies have greater effect than the old ones; 70% of the score is determined by whatever has happened within the past 2 years.

Watch out for Fair Debt Collection Practices Act (FDCPA) Violations

The law is on your side when it comes to the manner in which the debt collection agencies can collect debts from you. If they violate these, you can actually compel them to delete your derogatory entries since the penalties they will pay far exceed the amount that might be outstanding (some fines could go as high as $10,000). Actually, every violation has a penalty of $1000 payable to you! Here are some of the things to watch out for.

- If the creditor calls you before 8.00 am in the morning
- If they call after 9.00 pm
- If they call you at your place of work persistently
- If they call third parties. Creditors are only allowed to call your spouse apart from you for purposes of tracing you.
- If they inform someone else and inform them that they are trying to recover debt from you.
- If they call you after you have officially notified them not to call you.
- If they contact you after you have officially informed them that you are being represented by an attorney.

You can effectively defend yourself by reporting to the FDCPA if you are subjected to the following:

*If they try to collect invalid debt. This happens more frequently than most people know. It happens due to various reasons; some are deliberate while others are accidental. Some collection agencies try to take advantage and attempt to do a double collection

*If a collection agency agent lies or uses deceptive language.

NB: Since the use of the term deceptive is quite vague, you can take advantage and get yourself off the hook.

*If a debt collector leaves unclean messages on your answering machine. If they leave such a message, they must state that they are trying to collect debt. They must also leave their name and the name of the agency they are acting for.

*If they sue or threaten to sue after 4 years lapse after you attended to a debt. Note that the duration may differ in CA and a few other states.

*If they threaten and refer to being connected to a government agency courts or any law enforcement agent.

*When they threaten to sue you when they have no intention of doing so.

*If they threaten to garnish your income without explaining the due process. A creditor is supposed to file a suit and obtain judgment before they can garnish the income of debtors.

*If they sue you in another place other than where you live now and where you agreed

All you have to do to start the process is to tell them that you have been recording all their calls.

Chapter 5: How to Convert Bad Credit into Good Credit

Debunking eight common credit score myths

Loans have become a great tool that helps people solve their financial issues in no time. Although, beyond the several advantages and responsibilities, there are certain myths that we must be aware of and break. If you have plans to acquire a loan but are not sure if it's your best option, this book will show you how to see and handle the situation exactly as you should.

While some of us like credit score as it has favored us in our ability to handle it well, others see it as one that does more harm than good, which is not the case. The issue with people who do not enjoy the credit score is because they were misinformed on some things and it leads them to fall into traps they could have avoided if they had the right information all along. That's why in this section of this book, we will be discussing the eight common myths to break on credit score. These myths are:

1. When you close your many credit accounts, your credit score will improve

This may seem logically sound but is completely false. The way credit scores are calculated in parts is known as credit/ debt ratio. The agencies who calculate your score evaluate the amount of debt that you have and the amount of credit that is available for you to draw.

So let's assume you have ten credit cards and the credit availability all sums up to $100,000 and you have used only $15,000 of that available credit, your credit utilization rate becomes 15%. This is known as positive since you have 85% of your unused credit.

Let's take a case of you closing seven accounts because you're not using them. You will still have $15,000 in debt, but in this case, your sum total credit now available drops to $30,000. This means that your credit utilization rate has skyrocketed by 50%, hence your credit score dropping.

Do not close credit cards like this. It is better to put the cards away safely. And if there's a chance you can increase your credit limit, go for it. As long as you are not maximizing it, it will help your credit score.

2.   Once you have a bad credit score, it is impossible to get loans or credits

This myth has been derived from advertisements that require a good credit score to get funding. Interestingly, almost everyone can get funding no matter what their credit score may be, whether it is increased in the 800s or lower in the 400s.

What a credit score represents to financial institutions is a level of risk as this determines, to a large extent, the terms of any loan or credit received. Let's say, for example, someone who has a credit score of 800; the individual will be considered low risk for the financial institution. They already know that this person pays in good time, has available credit in high quantity and has longevity with his accounts. This will hence result in a low-interest rate and more credit available.

However, someone with a credit score of 450 will be considered high-risk. The reason is that the loans and credits will be available but will have oppressive interest rates for very little credits.

3.   Credit scores tend to change only a few times a year

Credit scores are usually in constant change. The information with which you calculate your score is derived from the financial institutions you maintain business relationships with. If you miss making a payment, it will reflect almost immediately. If you go ahead to close multiple accounts, the information will have an impact on your score much earlier than 3 or 6 months.

Looking at your credit score now, you can be able to see the latest updates that have been made. The time actually varies as sometimes it can be a matter of hours, than days or even weeks. Knowing this, you should ensure to check your credit score on a regular basis. So in case something bad happens, you can address it early enough.

4.   One thing that affects your score is the amount of money you make.

This is so not true. Your credit score does not list the employers' income but rather the credit accounts. So regardless of what you earn a year, whether you're a CEO who earns 3 million a year or an entry-level worker who earns $30,000 a year, your income does not determine your credit score. Interestingly, a wealthy CEO, even with so much money, might have a bad credit score because of bankruptcy or successions of late payments in the previous years.

The only way that your income can affect your credit score is if you live a Champagne lifestyle and having only a beer budget. That can be financially unhealthy for you. If it happens that you run out of your cards, by making minimum payments and losing them completely, your score gradually becomes a great success and peaks the top, as it should.

5.   Bringing a balance to your credit card also helps your score

No, not at all. To be quite frank, it doesn't hurt that either. But you would be wrong to think that keeping money on your card helps your score because it really doesn't. Ideally, I advise you to pay the balances on your cards fully every month in order to avoid paying interest on purchases. If you're just paying the minimum, then you're not doing yourself any good and wasting your money. Most of this minimum payment can be paid to the credit card company as only a small fraction pays the balance.

Do not bring a balance whenever possible. And if your balance exceeds 30% of your card, you should consider transferring from half to another card. When one-third of the credit is used on a card, then that can actually damage the credit score. In an ideal case, the balance ought to be less than 30% of the credit available; the lower it is, the better for you. This will be a good place to request a credit line increase, so as your line is increased by a few thousand dollars, your balance is affected and falls below 30%, hence increasing your credit score.

6. You can have an excellent credit report if you have no credit

The lack of credit is a good thing in some countries but not in the US. If you have never had a credit card or a car loan, you must be financially responsible. But as for the United States, your credit history determines your credit score. Good credit history equals a good credit score and vice versa.

All in all, credit scores are built. Financial institutions who lend loans and credits want to know that you will borrow money and payback on time coupled with an interest. Once they see that, then you are safe from any risk.

7. You can't recover from a bad credit score. It stays with you for life.

If you currently have a poor credit score, it is not the end of the world. If you are paying exorbitant interest rates now, you won't be doing so forever. Although repairing and rebuilding take time and patience.

Stick with the basics and be consistent with it. Open new credit lines and pay your credit card bills in time. Try to never miss a payment. Make your balances low at all times. Keep a very steady but low credit usage ratio. Do not apply to many cards or accounts in a year.

Once you can do these, even amidst all financial difficulties, your credit score will change for better.

145

CATEGORY	SCORE
Excellent (30% of People)	750 - 850
Good (13% of People)	700 - 749
Fair (18% of People)	650 - 699
Poor (34% of People)	550 - 649
BAD (16% of People)	350 - 549

Chapter 6: 7 Quickest and Easiest Strategies to Raise Your Score

Pay off what you owe

While this is going to be easier said than done in most situations, according to Experian, the ideal amount of credit utilization that you want is 30 percent or less. While there are other ways to increase your credit utilization rating, paying off what you owe on time each month will also go towards showing you can pay your bills on time, essentially pulling double duty when it comes to improving your credit score. It will also make it easier to follow through on the following tips.

Pay Bills The Day You Get Them

This might take some discipline but it's a great system to stay on track - pay your bills on the same day they arrive in the mail. If you have online banking, this will be quite easy: the bill arrives, you go to your computer or smart phone and log into your bank account, and you pay your bill. Done. One less thing on your mind and zero risk of being late with the payment.

Very often we are lulled into a false realty by bill due dates that are weeks away. You look at your account and think: I have a thousand bucks in there. Meanwhile you have three bills laying around for half of that amount. Your discretionary spending (wants, not needs) is quite different when you think you have X amount in your account rather than X minus bills. By paying your bills right away, you get them out of the way and won't forget to pay them. You are also going to spend less money because your account will be a more honest reflection of your financial picture.

It is incredible how easy it is to get into trouble financially when everything is payable in a month. We lose touch with where we really stand in terms of money. If you cannot afford to pay every bill as it comes in, maybe take out a small loan to bring you to square one, and then chip away at the loan.

Get A Cash Secured Loan

Similar to the secured credit card, you can build and repair credit by taking out a cash secured loan. In this case, offer the bank to borrow x amount and use that amount as collateral on the loan. The funds will be locked down in a savings account and you will gain access to the borrowed funds once the loan is paid in full.

The advantage to the bank is that they have zero risk (they repay the loan with the savings if the deal goes south), they make a profit on the deal since the rate they pay on savings deposit is lower than the rate you pay on the loan, and the loan officer is happy about getting another sale. A good idea is to borrow an amount like $5,000 to $10,000 and repay it over the next 3 to 5 years with regular scheduled payments. As long as there are no late payments, this will count as a positive on your credit history. Do not repay the loan immediately, as you want the loan to run for a long time for maximum effect.

If the loan is repaid within a few months, it might not even have a chance of making a good impact on your credit score. As a bonus, once the loan is paid off, you will have access to the savings. This is often done by some creative lenders to help young people build credit and can be a forced savings plan for a future home purchase down payment.

Negotiate To Repay Written Off Items

Sometimes our mistakes are in the past and we are still paying for them in the present. Unpaid collections and written off loans and credit card balances not only look horrible on your credit history, they also lower your credit score immensely.

A write-off is basically when the lender decides that they have no chance of recovering the amount owed to them by you. They write-off the amount on their books and inform the credit bureaus. If you are able to do so, you should seriously consider paying any written off debts that you may have. You can often do so at favorable terms.

Call up the company that wrote off the debt and inform them that you would like to make amends by paying back some or all of the debt you owed them and that was written off. This will basically be free money for them as they have already made provisions for the loss. It makes the manager look good. Your condition should be that once the written off debt has been repaid by you, they will have to report to the credit bureaus and inform them of the change. Get this in writing and forward a copy of the letter to the credit bureaus. This will erase the negative entry on your credit history and make your credit score shoot upwards. If you are brave, you can also try to negotiate the amount it will take to remove the write off. Ask them to reverse any fees that might have been added over the course of the debt being delinquent. Sometimes they will also remove accrued interest from the debt and aim to recover only the initial amount owed to them less any payments made. You can also just bluff and say you only have x amount and are willing to pay that to them in return for the credit history adjustment. Sometimes, they will think that 40% recovered is better than 0% and go for it.

The point of all of this is that these things are not permanent and can be fixed if you are willing to make the effort.

When Rate Shopping, Do It Quickly

Every time there is an inquiry on your credit history, your score drops by about 10 points. If you are buying a new car or applying for a mortgage, you are likely to approach a few different lenders in order to get the best rate. Often their pricing is dependent on your credit score and they will need to view your credit history first before providing a quote.

When you are applying at only one bank, an inquiry is fine and won't affect your credit score much. It becomes messy though, when you have five or six different bankers taking a look over an extended period of time (one every weekend for instance). The credit bureaus understand that you might have to go through this process in order to get the best rate possible, they will not penalize you for multiple inquiries within a short period of time.

There is no specific time period in which to rate shop, but generally you don't want to be looking around for more than a week. Two weeks at the most if you want to take a risk.

Keeping all credit inquiries to within a short time period is a little easier done for mortgages since a house purchase is usually a very planned out process, and you can therefore stack a few mortgage appointments in one week. It is much harder when buying a car and applying for car loans to keep within a short time period. You might get pre-approved at your local bank, but then get roped into financing through the dealership when you finally find the right car a few weeks later. The local bank will pull a credit history and the dealership will send the loan application out to multiple lender, who will all likely look at the credit history again.

In order to avoid taking multiple hits to your credit score, try to wrap up your rate and loan shopping in a short period of time. There are also many banks out there that do not price your rate based on your credit score - these banks will be able to quote you a rate without pulling your credit history first. Once you officially apply for the loan, they will review the credit history for underwriting.

Avoid Over-Extending Yourself

People who live within their means usually have great credit. People who want to buy everything, and borrow every penny possible, usually have lousy credit. If you borrow too much, you will eventually run into problems making the payments. You can have a lot of debt and decent credit at the same time, but someday something might happen and cause the whole house of cards to fall down.

Often it takes a long time until problems become really obvious. Many people who have overextended themselves will keep things afloat for a while, usually by borrowing more and more. First they will forgo saving for retirement, then maintaining the house, then suddenly there is only enough to make the bare minimum payments on the credit cards and soon new debt is taken out to pay for old debt.

Banks will bail you out as often as they can because your banker is only a human and does not want to push you off the cliff. They will bail you out by giving more credit, and then some more until the day comes when there is no more room left. When that moment comes, the wall goes up and you are alone. Soon payments start coming in late and your credit score takes a nose dive. Once your credit history takes a hit, the chance of getting bailed out is going get even smaller.

For excessive debt to cause a lower credit score, you don't even need to be behind on payments. The amount you have borrowed and the level of usage of revolving credit, such as credit cards and lines of credit, can cause a drop in your score. At some point the credit bureau computer catches on that the big credit card balances aren't really going down month over month. It might just decide the you are in over your head and reward you with a lower score to scare away the lenders.

Set rules for yourself and your family when it comes to borrowing. You can't really avoid a mortgage, but things such as car purchases and vacations should have rules. When buying a car, try to buy the whole thing cash. If that is not possible, aim to have at least a 15% down payment on the purchase price. If you can't even come up with that, maybe you need to wait or buy a cheaper car. Boats, snowmobiles, motorcycles: these are toys and you really should not borrow 100% of the purchase price to buy them. The same goes for vacations: don't borrow money to go on vacation. If you already did, don't borrow for the next vacation before you have paid off the previous one.

These borrowing rules suck and they are no fun, but they will put you on much better financial footing and help you avoid the kind of overspending that will lead to credit problems.

Learn To Budget

Budgeting is a pain in the rear, even for people who are doing great financially. It is boring and it is restrictive, it sucks the life blood right out of you. Reaching or exceeding your monthly allowance for restaurant meals in a week is not fun. And where do unexpected dentist expenses go? What about roof repairs?

In many years as a lender for a bank I have given out hundreds of booklets on budgeting and personally given advice on the subject. There is a psychological barrier that make budgets so difficult. Everyone thinks they need to be perfect and on budget all the time, and once you go over your budget in even the least important category you feel like you broke your perfect record. Once perfection has been tainted, the baby is thrown out with the bathwater and the habit of budgeting is abandoned. Maybe abandoning your budget reinforces your belief that budgets are hard and you are bad with money. You need to get past this and do your best to stick with it.

Budgets are like Bootcamps for fat kids. There is that sick feeling at first when your body is woken up to reality. Then there are all the steps that follow that you just keep on messing up on and never really getting perfect. Then there is the cheating every once in a while when you somehow manage to get your hands on a bag of chips. After it's all said and done, it was no fun, you didn't do everything perfectly, but you still walked away a little better or even much better than before.

The point of a budget is to put everything down on paper. How much money is coming in every month? How much money is going out. Is less money going out than coming in but you are still going further into debt? Then you either missed a few items or are not totally honest with yourself, you will need to start again. Just knowing how razor thin the margin is between how much is coming in and how much is going out, might stop you from buying that cookbook that you will never use. Sit down and do your budget and be brutally honest. You don't even need to consciously try to save money, you subconsciously start spending less

.

Break your spending into different categories and decide how much you should spend on each category. Figure out the costs that you cannot change, such as rent or mortgage payments or car insurance. Then figure out what your discretionary spending is, these are the things that are wants and not needs. Those are the categories that you can save money on. Set a budget and try to hit it. Celebrate every time you decide not to spend money.

Whenever you are less than perfect with your budgeting, don't be too hard on yourself. The idea of your budget is for you to be aware of where your money is going, and of where it should be going. Even if you stick to the budget only 2% of the time, you're still better off than not having a budget at all and sticking to it 0% of the time. Every little bit counts.

Authorized users

If you don't have the credit to get a new credit card, or even to extend your current credit line, then your best choice may be to find someone you trust and ask them to become an authorized user on their card. While most people will likely balk at the idea, you may be able to pacify them by explaining that you don't need a copy of their card or have any intent on using it, simply being listed on the card is enough to improve your credit utilization rating. Not only that, but you will also get credit for the on-time payments that this other person makes as well.

Open a new account

Improving your credit utilization rate is one of the best ways to start rebuilding your credit. If your current credit card company won't increase your credit limit you may way to try applying for another credit card instead. If your credit is not so hot then your rates are going to be higher, but this won't matter as long as you don't plan on using the card in the first place. Remember, credit utilization rate is a combination of your total available lines of credit so this can be a good way to drop your current utilization rate substantially, especially if you won't be able to pay off what you currently owe for a significant period of time.

Keep in mind, however, that if you choose this route then you are only going to want to apply for one new card every couple of months, especially if you aren't sure if you are going to be approved, as too many hard credit inquiries will only cause your credit score to drop, even if you do end up with a better credit utilization rate as a result. Spreading out these requests will give the inquiries time to drop off naturally and will prevent you from looking desperate to potential lenders which can also make it more difficult to get a new card.

Increase your credit limit

If you aren't currently in a position to pay down your credit card balance, you can still improve your credit utilization rate by increasing your current credit limit. This is an easy way to improve your credit utilization rate without putting any more money out up front. If you do this, however, it is important that you don't take advantage of the increased credit line as if you find yourself up against the limit again you will be worse off than when you started. Only pursue this option if you have the willpower to avoid racking up extra charges, especially if you are already strapped when it comes to the payments you need to make each month; decreasing your credit utilization limit while also making more late payments is a lateral move at best.

Pay your credit card bills twice a month

If you have a credit card that you use on a regular basis, say for example because it offers you reward points, so much so that you max it out each month, it may actually be hurting your credit even though you pay it off in full at the end of each month. This may be the case due to the way the credit card company reports to the credit bureau; depending on when they report each month it could show that your credit utilization rate is close to 100 percent depending on what your credit line currently is, thus hurting your credit score. As such, paying off your credit card in two smaller chunks throughout the month can actually help boost your credit without costing you anything extra overall.

Chapter 7: How to Get out of Debt

Being in debt can hold you back from achieving financial success and happiness. Credit card debts, in particular, are high interest debts that can pose serious threats to your financial security if allowed to balloon to uncontrollable levels. If you are deeply in debt, you have to face the problem and figure out how you can settle your liabilities as quickly as possible. Work out a repayment plan and be firm on your resolve to get out of debt fast. Stay motivated by constantly reminding yourself of the rewards and benefits of being debt-free.

Here are good reasons why you should pay off your debts fast and stay debt-free for life:

1. Being debt-free means you have full control over your finances. You will no longer be at the mercy of your creditors.

2. You will have the money to send your kids to great schools, buy the car you want, or live comfortably in your dream house.

3. Being debt-free means you can use your income to enjoy the finer things in life.

4. Not having to worry about payment and payment due dates reduces anxiety and stress and helps you live a happier and healthier life.

5. By staying out of debt, you will have more money to save and invest for your retirement.

6. You will be in a better position to prepare for your children's future and deal with life's challenges.

    When you set your sights on higher goals, it becomes easier to make sacrifices for a few months or years in exchange for a lifetime of financial security and abundance.

Strategies to Get Out of Debt

How you will settle your debt will depend on your actual financial situation and preferences. Here are proven strategies you can consider when deciding on a payment plan:

1. Make a list of everything you owe. Write down the creditor's name, loan balance, interest rate, and minimum monthly payment required.

2. Sort your debts by amount and interest rate. This will help you assess what credit card debt(s) to prioritize. The most popular method is to put more payment into the debt account with the higher interest rate while paying the minimum amount on the rest of the loans. Once this debt is fully paid, you can continue to use the extra fund to pay off the next card on the list. Using this method can help you pay your debts faster.

3. Another popular strategy is to prioritize payment for the card(s) with the lowest balance while paying the rest of the creditors the minimum amount due. This strategy can be a powerful morale booster. After paying the first target debt in full, you can use the extra fund towards the payment of the card with the next lowest balance.

4. Negotiate with your creditors for a lower rate. If your credit standing is good, banks will likely agree to give you a lower rate instead of losing your account to another creditor. You can use the savings from the reduced interest rate to pay off your principal loan.

5. Consolidating your debts and doing a balance transfer at a significantly lower rate are other options you can consider to free yourself from debt and at the same time help you save on interest charges. You can do this by asking one of your existing creditors to absorb loan balances from your other cards. Another way to consolidate your loans is by opening a new

credit line with a new lender and transferring your loan balances to this new account.

6. Avoid borrowing money to pay your debts or minimum monthly payments. Your goal is to free yourself from debt as fast as possible.

7. Immediately after establishing your emergency fund, prioritize debt payment and use any extra cash, bonuses, or tax refunds to pay down your debts. You will save big on interest charges by using your unexpected funds to settle your debts faster.

8. Don't use your credit cards to purchase new items or pay for your household expenses just because you have managed to free a portion of your card balance.

9. Once you have paid off a credit card debt, have your account closed and cut your credit card. If you must maintain a credit card for contingencies while you're still in the process of building your emergency fund, just maintain one card and keep it in a place where you don't have easy access to it.

10. Don't use your home as guarantee for the payment of your credit card balances. Remember that credit cards are unsecured debts and are given to you on the basis of your credit scores. If you fail to pay, you risk losing your home.

11. You can negotiate with your creditors and banks directly. You don't have to hire the services of a debt settlement company or financial agents to arrange a balance transfer. Educate yourself on simple financial calculations and be able to compare banks' offers on your own.

12. Constantly visualize yourself as living the life of your dreams because you have finally conquered debt.

13. Finally, to pay off your debts faster, free off more funds by controlling your expenses and making more money.

Chapter 8: Avoid These Mistakes While Repairing Credit

For many people, a credit card is merely a convenient way to make transactions. However, few people realize that the little plastic card also has the ability to wreak havoc on their lives if not used carefully. Ultimately, misusing your credit account can destroy your credit scores and ultimately hamper your credit.

One way to prevent the damages that poorly handled credit can cause is to know about the mistakes that people commonly make and learn how to avoid them.

Paying just the minimum

Issuers of credit cards set a minimum amount that you should pay every billing period. Some people have the wrong notion that this is a godsend because it is so small compared to the total amount. They couldn't be more wrong.

Paying just the minimum amount on your credit card debt will not only increase the time it takes to pay off your balance, but it would also accrue more interest. In addition, your credit score would suffer because as your balance grows, your credit utilization grows as well and that has a negative effect on your credit score.

To avoid having to pay more in the long run, try to pay the total balance every billing cycle. Don't let it accrue interest.

Ignoring Your Billing Statement

If you don't check your credit card's billing statement often, the more likely it is that you'll risk missing payment or paying less than you should have for it to be considered on time.

In addition, ignoring your card's statement will cause you to miss some important announcements, such as an announcement to the changes on your credit card's terms.

Make it a habit to check your billing statement because it will often be your guide to know if there are any false activities on your account. Besides, doing so will help you keep your spending in check.

To make sure that the payments have been correctly applied to your account, or if the all the charges are accurate, always check your card's billing statement.

Failure to report a lost or stolen credit card immediately

The longer you take to file a report about your lost credit card, the longer the thief or the one who has gotten your card has to charge up your credit account.

If you immediately report your missing card before any false charges are made, the sooner you'll avoid possible responsibilities you have to deal with for the said charges. The sooner you report a missing credit card, the sooner it would limit your liabilities for false charges.

Canceling Your Credit Card

Now that you have finally paid off all your credit card bills which have been stressing you out for ages, your first impulse might be to get rid of your credit card as soon as possible, which is usually done by cutting up your card and closing your account.

But don't be too quick on doing that, as closing down your account so suddenly can actually lower your credit score. Keep in mind that the age of your accounts affects your credit scores.

Even if you have paid off your credit card, it would be much better for you if you just leave your credit account open, that is until you are 100% sure that you can offset the possible reduction in credit score by making changes that would boost it. Just keep it open and maintain low utilization.

Paying Late

Always pay for your monthly payments on time. If you keep on forgetting about your due dates, then you should come up with a system that can remind you about them. For example, you can set up auto pay with your bank or use apps to set reminders. If the primary reason is inconvenience, then organize your bills so you could schedule the best time to pay all if not most of them.

If you keep on paying late for your monthly payments, it can cost you for up to $38 in late fees, which will also depend on the number of times you have been late for the past 6 months.

Also, falling behind your payments for more than 30 days will also affect your credit score. But if your existing payment is more than 60 days late, then your card's issuer may raise your interest rate up to the penalty rate available.

Loaning your credit card

When you loan your credit card to another person, you will no longer have control over the purchases that they are about to make.

In the end, you'll still be responsible for paying all the bills, even if the person who borrowed your card doesn't pay you for the expenses.

Never ever loan your card to someone, even if it's someone you know, except if you are prepared to take responsibility to pay for the purchases that they are about to make.

Not Knowing Your Credit Card Terms

If you know how your credit card company handles the late payments, you'll be more likely to pay for your card's bill on time. After all, you'll know exactly how much they cost you.

166

Letting your card get charged-off

Acquiring a charge-off is one of the worst things that can happen to your credit card report and credit score. A charge-off will remain on your report for 7 years, and could significant affect your ability to get loans and credit cards several years in the future.

It would take about a total of 6 months of missed payments for you to be charged with a charge-off status. Before your card gets to that point, ensure your delinquent accounts are current.

Applying for too much credit

If you are on the checkout line and the cashier asked if you want to apply for a store credit card for the discount, do not accept it outright. You may love to have a discount on your purchases, but it is still a credit card. Remember that each time you apply for credit, an inquiry will show up on your credit report and will pull down your credit score a little. The discount you think you'll be getting might not be worth it.

Also, be careful about opening too many credit accounts if you plan on applying for big loans, such as mortgage, car loan, and others.

Maxing your card out

Utilizing more than 30% of your card's limit can be quite dangerous for your credit score. Also, by getting close to your credit's limit, it will put you at risk for fees that are over the limit, and even the penalty interest will increase your card's charges once you exceed your credit card's limit. Therefore, to have a manageable payment amount and healthy credit score, always maintain a good credit card balance.

Getting pressured into accepting new cards

Have you ever noticed that sometimes most of the letters in your mail are about new credit card offers? Or maybe you have encountered countless strangers who are calling you to pitch you one? Well, don't think that these are just your imagination, because they are not.

A lot of credit card companies send out millions or even billions of credit offers every year, but this doesn't mean that you have to accept all of their requests or listen to their sale pitches. You can freely choose to get out of the prescribed credit card offers and out of the credit card telemarketing lists.

You can also get out of the email and phone solicitations from the mortgages companies.

Sharing your credit card number with other people

Some credit card holders sometimes share their card's number to pay for a bill. But if someone calls, emails, or have mailed you with some requests and unsolicited personal information, such as your Social Security number or credit card number, never reveal it even if the person sounds legitimate or nice. These kinds of requests are part of financial scams that mostly target seniors. These fraudsters are trying to make unauthorized use of your good name and credit or steal your money.

If you do become a victim of identity theft, immediately report it to your Federal Trade Commission and to your local police department.

Paying tax bills with a credit card

If you don't pay for a federal tax debt, the IRS will have the power to tax your assets, put a right to claim or hold your property, or seize your tax refunds. However, none of it should intimidate you into paying them with your credit card.

The reason is that if you use your credit card, you will also have to pay for an interchange fee. This may run anywhere from 2% to 4% of the amount that you are paying for.

Now, add those to the 12% to 18% interest that you have to pay to your bank if you think of adding the tax charge to your balance. A better solution to your problem would be to set up a repayment plan with the IRS and pay your tax debts over time.

Applying for credit repair recklessly

If you have recently gone through a serious personal setback such as a foreclosure, divorce, or bankruptcy, your credit standing might be shaky or maybe even downright bad.

However, looking for a quick fix can actually put you in the hands of a con artist that specializes on tricking people i.e. charge you with hidden costs or high upfront fees for their fake services.

Also, be aware of companies or an individual that promises to "fix" your bad credit overnight. Fixing a really bad credit score won't happen overnight, it lasts for days, weeks, or maybe even a month if the process is slow.

Using your credit card to withdraw cash

Using credit cards to withdraw cash could be bad because the credit card issuer is not able to monitor the spending, and thus view it as a high-risk loan and subsequently charge higher interests.

If you don't fully pay off the amount you withdrew within a month, your balance will start racking up some interests. Therefore, you can quickly lose control over your debt if not handled as soon as possible, particularly if you only pay the minimum amount monthly.

Aiming for the "rewards"

We people have been known to use credit for all kinds of things, be it a lavish vacation or jewelry, or even cars and in some cases, expensive novelty products.

However, making large purchases on a credit card is definitely a no-no unless you are 100% sure that you can immediately pay off such large amounts in full.

Whatever benefits that you may gain, in terms of flier miles or hotel check-ins, will come with interest charges, which you'll have to pay if you don't immediately pay your balance off every month.

Ignoring Your Credit's Warning Signals

To improve your chances of getting a healthy credit rating, check your credit reports for free for at least once or twice a year from a government-mandated website. However, if you're in the process of building or rebuilding credit, that isn't just enough. Check it once a month. You may also want to sign up for credit monitoring services, among others.

Also take note of warning signs that indicate you might be in a debt trouble such as missing payments, only making minimum payments, regularly seeking for 0% card offers, a low-rate balance transfer just to afford payments, or charging without knowing how to pay for bills.

If any of the following warning signals are familiar to you, it's time you get your act together to start repairing your credit.

Financial Mistakes

Not building business credit

Many business owners are making big financial mistakes when it comes to business credit. One of the big mistakes is not building their business credit; they do not spend extra time and effort to build business and financial credibility for their business.

Not paying bills on time

Another major financial mistake business owners make is not paying their bills on time. In many cases, this lowers the business credit score, making it harder to get new credit at good terms.

Mixing personal and business credit

Another serious issue is the business owner mixing personal and business credit by using personal credit to pay for business debts. Investing personal credit and cash into the business is a big financial mistake. This may earn them trade credits, but those credits are not helpful in building business credit since they are not reported to the business credit reporting agencies.

Putting personal assets at risk to business debts

Using personal credit cards, cash, line of credit, etc. to pay business expenses creates a big financial issue as it puts the business owner's family assets at risk to business debts. When this happens, the business owner is creating personal liability by pledging personal assets rather than utilizing corporate credit

Most business owners do not manage their business credit, as they should, as an Asset rather than a Liability. A lot of business owners do not realize that business credit is an asset that grows with the business. A personal credit has a predetermined limit and borrowing ceiling, limiting what the business owner can be approved for. Building a strong business credit profile will help the business cash flow by reducing or improving vendor and supplier terms, credit card rates, financing costs and insurance premiums.

Chapter 9: How to Delete Bad Credit Legally

Public records that appear on your credit report include civil judgments, tax liens and bankruptcy filings.

Tax liens: the first thing you are going to want to do is to ensure that the debt has been paid in full. Next, you are going to want to go ahead and prepare to file a dispute. The federal government has a Fresh Start program that makes this process fairly straightforward. To qualify you are going to need to be current on your taxes and have received a Release of Tax Lien document. You will also need the original form that provided notice of the lien in the first place. You will then need to fill out IRS form 12277 Application for Withdrawal of Filed form 688Y, available at IRS.gov. You will then need to submit this, along with your original form and proof that you have paid off the lien to the IRS. You should then receive IRS form 10916(c) which states that the federal lien has been withdrawn. Finally, you will submit a copy of that form to the credit bureaus with a request that they remove the inaccurate information from your report.

Judgements: Having a judgement on your credit report can be nearly as harmful as having a repossession or a loan default. While removing a judgement is possible, it is not as easy as removing a late payment or a credit inquiry. A judgement shows up on your credit report if a judge signs off on a statement saying that you owe a specific debt. This occurs when a lawsuit is filed against you for the purpose of collecting a debt, even if you weren't aware of the court proceedings at the time. It is important to keep in mind that just because a judgement was issued against you, that doesn't mean the other party was paid, which is a fact that you will use to your advantage.

There are two different ways to deal with a judgement once it has hit your credit report, you can have the judgement dismissed, also known as vacated, or remove the judgment from your credit report.

Dismiss a judgement: In order to have a judgement dismissed, you need to file a motion to dismiss the judgment with the court that issued the judgement in the first place. This is essentially an appeal that states the original outcome was inaccurate or unfair based on a specific number of reasons. First you will want to look through the proceedings and ensure that the person who requested the judgement in the first place went ahead and followed all the correct procedures and laws for doing so in your area. If there was mismanagement of this process, the odds are that the judge didn't know about it when the judgement was made.

In addition to following up on the judgement process, you will need to ensure that the person filing the judgement also followed proper court proceedings as you may be able to win out based on a technicality. This is especially important if you failed to show up for your court date and the plaintiff won by default as long as you had a valid reason for not showing up for the hearing in the first place. Again, it is important to familiarize yourself with local laws for this process to be effective.

When you prepare your motion to vacate it is important you follow local rules for civil procedure to the letter, the rules for your area should spell out exactly what you need to do, explain valid reasons a judgment can be vacated and will often include specific language you will need to use to file your motion.

The document you create should explain why the judgement should be vacated, starting with the reasons why you are bringing the motion forward. You will need to state your procedural defense and explain why you missed the original hearing if that is what happened. Valid reasons include that you were not served properly, that you responded to the summons but there was no initial judgment or that you did not have time to make it to the hearing based on when you were served. There may be other valid reasons in your area as well.

You will also need to include reasons why the judgement would have been dismissed if you had been at the hearing including things like, the collection agency failed to respond to your validation request or that the debt amount exceed local usury interest limits.

Bankruptcy: Removing a bankruptcy from your credit report is the most difficult black mark to remove. While it is far from a sure thing, a general rule is that the older the bankruptcy is, the easier it is to remove. To get started you are going to want to look for errors relating to it, if there are then you are in luck. If you find errors you can go about asking the bureau to remove them in the standard way.

Regardless if the information is accurate or not, you are still going to want to ask the bureau to verify the bankruptcy as they will be unlikely to go about doing it in the right way. Assuming they come back and tell you that it has been verified by one court or another, this is almost always inaccurate as courts rarely verify bankruptcies. With this information in hand, you will want to reach out to the court that has been specified and ask them how they verify bankruptcies. You can call and ask for this information, typically from the clerk of the court. Assuming they explain that they don't verify bankruptcies you will then want to get that fact in writing.

When you receive this letter in the mail, you will then want to send it to the bureau that claimed to have verified your bankruptcy in the first place along with a letter explaining what it is and stating that, as the bankruptcy was not actually verified, you want it taken off your record as by not doing so previously, but saying that they did, they are in direct violation   of   the   FCRA.

Deletion of Negative Public Records (Judgments)

Ever had your wages garnished?

I did – I fought – I won

I had to pay a settlement, but I got the judgement VACATED from the clerk of court and removed completely from my credit record.

Garnishments are the worst thing for your credit, you don't want this on your report, and any potential employers will have a serious problem with this.

I used whatever leverage I could find and wrote a letter to the Judge that handled the case and explained in lengthy detail how it all happened, why the creditor was being too harsh and ruthless and what violations I believed the committed.

The Judge actually ruled in my favor for the second hearing which I could not attend due to work, I gave my letter to the bailiff before the court date.

I still had to pay court costs but I won. I wasn't even there, and the Creditor's attorney was very upset, apparently he losing the case really made him look bad to the firms' Partners.

Public Records will require serious measures to get vacated or deleted. Keep in mind anything is negotiable if you can find the leverage or violation within the Fair Credit Acts. Most of the time they are there, but you have to look very hard.

In addition, getting creditors to vacate or delete a public judgement can be accomplished with settlements and negotiations while leveraging the Fair Credit Acts. Where there is a will there is a way. Do you think attorneys give up when the odds are stacked against their case? No way, they find loopholes and any leverage they can find – I would suggest you view defending your credit report the same way, only the consumer laws are MORE biased for you.

Chapter 10: Right Mindset for Credit Management

Having the mindset of a lender allows you to manage your money in a way that makes you a good credit candidate in the eyes of lenders. Apply the following tips when handling your finances to help you develop the mindset of a lender.

1. Do your research.

Knowing how money works will go a long way toward helping you maintain your credit report's good standing. Keep your good credit score from dipping by reading books on finance management. It helps if you have knowledge on how your accounts and loans work so that handling them will be easier on you. When you take steps to understand how money works in general, you equip yourself with tools that will help you make wiser financial decisions and avoid a bad credit rating.

2. Confirm your closed accounts.

It doesn't matter if they are bank accounts, credit accounts, or even your utility company accounts – what does matter is that you ask for a written confirmation for every account you close. Make sure that each closed account has been fully paid up. It helps if you follow up with your bank or credit card company a couple of months afterwards to confirm that the accounts have been closed.

3. Know how lenders view you.

Your credit score is not the only thing that lenders will often examine in your credit report. They also take the time to look at other financial indicators such as your employment history, your income, and your savings. Work on keeping these details in order to help you maintain your good credit score and achieve good overall credit, especially since there are a number of lenders who employ their own methods of computing credit scores.

4. Constantly update your records, including your current address.

Making sure that all your records are updated regularly helps you keep your lenders and financial managers up-to-date as well. It helps to keep all of your financial information in one folder at home, including and especially your current address. It will serve as a reminder to contact your creditors in case you move and give them your new address. This will prevent the problems of not getting your bills, being unable to pay them, and seeing your credit score go down as a result.

5. Aim for stability.

As much as possible, do not move around too much. Moving frequently results in your having to switch banks. This prevents you from developing long-term relationships with any of them, and this has a negative effect on your credit score and credit report. On the same note, it helps to avoid changing jobs too often. To some lenders, frequent job changes is an indication that you are likely to make loan defaults or go off with the money without paying. It also helps to avoid frequently changing your credit accounts and credit companies. Doing so prevents you from building a good credit relationship with any of them and could cause you to have a low credit rating.

6. Keep the lines of credit communication open.

As soon as a problem in your finances crops up, take steps to talk to your creditors. This will give them reassurance about your being responsible as a borrower, and this helps to prevent your credit report from being negatively affected. All it takes is calling them over the phone and arranging to have your payment schedules adjusted, as well as getting your penalties waived free of charge.

Chapter 11: Financial Freedom

Developing Wealth

Positive Wealth Consciousness

Throughout the years through a research study, interviews, I've discovered that individuals who have an excellent deal of wealth and individuals who preserve a favorable capital have actually established a favorable wealth awareness.

I keep in mind talking to a buddy, who owns a chain of hotels across the United States and is now expanding into Canada and overseas. He explained he had actually originated from an immigrant family; his daddy worked as an accounting professional and later on opened a store while his mother put herself through school eventually ending up being a nursing sister. However, my point is he didn't have a family that provided him with a million dollars to start his endeavor. Rather he began off working for his father, ultimately took control of the company, bought another, made it a success offered it and purchased another till he got his first hotel just outside Dallas.

Lets define positive wealth consciousness as a method of believing that you can and will generate income. It involves thinking that it is your right to generate income and create wealth. It needs that you concentrate on all the great things that your wealth can do for you and those around you. If you have wealth, you will assist more individuals, and it means understanding that. It suggests putting your ego aside- not wanting wealth so that you can flaunt and say: "Look at me, I'm rich." Rather it suggests saying: "Yes, I have a lot of wealth which enables me to take care of a lot of people, including my household and all those that I help when I invest my money."

You will invest your money, let's face it , the more you have, the more you will spend.

In order to bring in wealth, you need to very first take a look at where you are now and then create a realistic approach for a couple of months,a year, or more years. Perhaps you are indebted due to the task-

181

intending to have a million dollars in 6 months is not being extremely realistic. Rather your very first priority must be to get and get a job out of debt. If you currently have a job and you want to make more cash then offer yourself some sensible targets for the next 3 months, 6 months, year, and 5 years. Now I understand a few of you will say it's tough to generate the income, I do not know what to do to make more money, I'm in debt and don't understand how to go out. For each issue, there is an option of solution otherwise, we would not have problems. Concentrate on finding an option. Train your mind to focus on the service. Begin to forward messages to your conscious mind for a solution. Do this frequently, and you'll get answers. The money will not fall from the sky, but you will be guided to it. How Do You Train Your Mind? You initially focus on what you desire. Let's state you wish to find a task- you start to proclaim that you know what to do to find a task.

What You Can Do To Attract Wealth

There are a variety of techniques you can employ to attract wealth, regardless of your situation. You have to get your mind to work for you and not versus you. Here's a little exercise you can do. Get a notepad and a pen. Now begin thinking of generating income or enhancing your financial resources. Jot down all the thoughts that come to mind when you think of enhancing your finances or creating wealth. Be sincere – then you will see this list. Keep going until you feel you have had to satisfy. Keep contributing to that list throughout the day. Then when you feel you have got enough - have a look at what you wrote. Highlight the thoughts that are favorable and circle the ideas that are negative. How lots of are you negative? Any negative thought that you have about money or to improve your finances is connected to a belief that you have about money and only works against you. If you believe it's challenging to make more cash, you'll only have problems when it concerns making cash. Why? Due to the fact that your subconscious mind is just going to develop your truth based on your beliefs. If these beliefs are bad or great for you, it doesn't care. It simply acts upon your guidelines, and those guidelines are your beliefs and thoughts. To alter your thoughts and you change your beliefs. Modify your beliefs, and you change your life.

Chapter 12: The FUQ'S (Frequently Unasked Questions): Things Everyone Should Know About Their Credit Score.

Frequently Unasked Questions

In life, questions are more important than answers. The reason is that you get a clearer understanding of things when you learn to ask the right questions. So, I called this the Frequently Unasked Questions because this section deals with questions that people want to ask about but is not really what everybody asks, so they assume it is not necessary to know. Just like I have mentioned over and over again in this book, the best way to understand the credit score world is to never assume you know it all. Keep asking and researching, find out information about your credit report, credit score and how banks make use of your credit history in deciding on your loan requests. Here, I will show you questions you may already know the answers to, but I will take my time to properly explain them and also questions you might have never even thought of yet, but I bet you they will be useful in the long-run.

What is the catch in having a good score?

Everyone should be interested in having a good score as this has several advantages. Some of which are, for a case where you would like to take a loan out, it will help you get very favorable conditions. This also supports you in winning the contract for a new apartment. Many property managers do not take the risk and look for solvent tenants in particular who pay the rent on time. These are just a few benefits, amongst many.

What factors influence my credit rating?

When you're shopping, either online or in a fixed shop or supermarket, there's a lot to consider. "Zero percent financing" sounds like a good idea, but bear in mind that this is also a loan. This is not often concluded with the company, where a product is to be bought, but with a cooperating bank. Because "zero-percent financing" is a loan, it is only available to consumers with good credit ratings and has an impact on your score. Paying attention to some hidden costs such as processing fee which is also very important. Either it is online or on the ground, when ordering from mail-order companies, endeavor to pay invoices on time. Otherwise, your score can be affected negatively. A corresponding score means that you can't order on account.

What is the importance of performing scoring procedures?

The scoring procedures are performed most times when you want to borrow. Even if you're using the "zero-percent financing," a scoring is carried out nevertheless. Moreover, the scoring plays a major role if a company is to provide a service before you pay for it. This often happens with mobile phone contracts or shipping dealers a lot. However, the score value does not only determines whether a loan is granted to you but on what terms and conditions as well. A customer with a good score will obviously receive better terms and conditions than a customer with a bad one. They can, therefore, be able to ascertain that the customer will repay the credit without hitch or difficulty. This then means that scoring procedures help companies, banks and as well as service providers, in particular, to assess the risk of a business and be able to hedge it.

How do they compose my personal score?

The scoring process involves, on one part, one's personal data and historical experience on the other. From this, a phantom score is prepared by means of mathematical-statistical methods, allowing indications of the future behavior of the "scanned" person. Including the data and experience values, already included in the evaluation, the socio-demographic data (such as gender, age, the payment experience, known address, etc.) or contract data (such as the number of accounts and credit cards). However, the specific composition of scoring is a whole lot different for each scoring provider and is not made public.

Are credit rating and credit scoring the same?

No, they aren't. Score values deal with the creditworthiness of a group of people. However, the term "creditworthiness" or credit rating is known as the solvency of an individual or a company.

What does scoring entail?

Scoring helps to predict the behavior of groups of people with similar characteristics. Mathematical-statistical methods are used to calculate scores of a group of people and hence a statement is obtained on the risk of payment default of those people. The assumption most times is that people with the same characteristics will also tend to behave the same manner. Hence, this suggests that scores do not evaluate the creditworthiness of a single person, but rather predicts the payment behaviors of a group of people to which a specific person belongs to. In the scoring process, empirical values from the past are applied to make deductions on similar events that play out in the future.

What time was credit scoring born?

Around the late 1950s and early 1960s, banks in the United States of America started working together by sharing their customer data, which included account balances and payment histories especially.

This method was, at first, limited to just small communities.

However, as of the 1970s, several large companies emerged as leaders in credit reporting.

In 1970, the American Congress initially approved the Fair Credit Reporting Act (FCRA) in order to control the manner in which credit verification companies handled personal consumer information. This was the first step towards the regulation of the sector.

In the early 1980s, loans, requests, detailed personal information (including social security numbers, addresses, date of birth) and also payments that are still the basis of the credit valuation was electronically stored.

Why credit scoring? Why does it exist?

The credit history reporting system aids banks in not lending money to customers who have already been over-exposed and tagged as bad payers.

Until less than 80 years ago, the banking sector was a different experience entirely. Then, if you want to borrow money, you had to go into a bank branch and convince a manager one-on-one to grant you a loan. A proof of your income would have been requested from you as well as personal references who could guarantee your reliability. Back then, most loans were taken care of by guarantees, meaning that good collateral had to be offered to pay off the loan.

The commonest example of a loan guaranteed today is the loan for buying a property. In this agreement, the property is still the one that acts as the collateral.

With time, the high availability of credit cards as a comfortable electronic purchasing tool has also cleared the unsecured loan. And even if the unsecured loan were more profitable to banks, it was still very risky because there would be no guarantee for the bank to repay the sum paid if the debtor does not repay the loan.

Because of this, the credit scoring system came into play and was created to enable banks to have a central source of information on prospective customers.

What are the other factors that influence your credit scoring?

Yes, some of which are the average age of your current accounts, recent funding requests and any collateral that has been pledged against your assets.

Each of these makes up about 10-15% of your credit score.

The longer you have the current account, the better. Also, try to limit the credit requests to no more than two at least every six months. When you have too many credit requests in a short time, it can decrease your credit score as it suggests that you are in desperate need of money.

However, there is an exception for those whose credit requests are of the same nature. This will indicate that you are making an evaluation of a particular expense.

If it happens that these requests occur within a month or so, it will be generally accepted as one request.

What does the personal information in my credit scoring consist of exactly?

Your credit scoring contains all information about you, which includes your name, social security number, address and information about your financial assets, such as payments histories, balances and loan applications.

Your credit report majorly contains detailed information on recent activity on your financial accounts. This includes:

Credit requests: whenever you request a credit, either you have been approved or not.

Open loans: the data will have the bank, the loan amount, the loan opening date, the monthly payment amount and the payment history.

Use of credit cards: data includes the ban, credit limit, account opening date, payment history and the monthly payment amount.

Closed accounts: a closed account remains on the report for a maximum of up to seven years.

Public accounts: include judicial decisions and bankruptcy declarations.

How do you know you are doing a good job? How do you measure your progress?

As much as your credit report contains all information about your credit history, your credit score remains the best way to measure your progress in building your credit. Your credit score is referred to as the numerical summary of all information contained in your credit report within a particular time. It is the number that lenders and creditors use to decide whether to approve your requests and what interest rate to charge.

There are sites on which you can get your scores free of charge, some of which are creditkarma.com and creditsesame.com. You can also get your for FICO number for an affordable fee at myFICO.com. This FICO score, especially, is the one most creditors use.

This way, you can regularly monitor your credit score and update yourself on the changes that occur over time in your credit history.

How can I repair my bad credit scoring?

It's the same method for building a good one! Paying bills on time and staying away from debts. The best way to repair your credit is to pay your bills, reduce the level of debt per time and limit demand for fresh loans.

It would take about one or two years of responsible credit management to see your credit score improve exponentially. There are no shortcuts. Stick with this and you will see the change you desire

Chapter 13: Business Credit Cards

Whenever you attempt to open up a new business, you will need some funding to cover a lot of its initial expenses. Your personal credit card will be sufficient to start the business but only to a point. If the business you are planning to set up is of a certain size, you might want to apply for a business credit card.

What are business credit cards and what makes them different?

A business credit card shares mostly the same functions with a typical personal credit card. You use them to make transactions and pay for the charges each card makes at the end of the month. However, there are certain aspects that make a business credit card considerably different from your typical card.

1. It's Not Covered by Most Consumer Protection Laws

This is quite simple: under the law, businesses are of a different category from what you will call "consumers". Sure, you can tell yourself that you yourself are a consumer but the credit card was issued for the legal entity that makes up your business.

This means that certain consumer protection laws like the Credit Card Act of 2009 won't apply to you as the card holder. This could lead to a number of problems which will include sudden shifts in that card's Annual Percentage Rate, even overnight at some instances, and charges for penalties and fees that border on being expensive and unreasonable. However, there is a silver lining to all of this. If your business is quite small, some consumer protection laws might be extended to you. This is not true for all issuers so it's best not to expect to be covered once you are issued the card.

2. Higher Credit Limits

Due to the fact that your business is going to make a lot of expenses, the starting credit limit for a business credit card tends to be higher compared to personal ones. As such, if you can expect your business to make a lot of notable transactions, it's best that you apply for a credit card for businesses so you don't max your cards out quickly.

Of course, the same things that affect your credit score as a private individual will also affect you as the business owner. Even with the higher credit limit, the system of credit utilization rates still apply. Any credit you have available on that card, then, will be compared to the credit that you actually use on a regular basis. Depending on the reporting agency, credit utilization may comprise 30% to 40% of your score.

If you are not the type to overly rely on your business credit card, this could be an advantage for you. The higher credit limit means that it will take several huge purchases for you to even reach the 30% threshold reporting agencies recommend credit card users stick to. So as long as your credit utilization is within 15% to 19%, your credit score should remain high.

3. It Affects All Credit, Both Business and Personal

When it comes to being a business owner, the distinction between your personal credit and the business's credit is often blurred. In other words, your personal credit can affect how the business itself can apply for and use credit.

For instance, when issuers look at your application for a business credit card, they would look at your personal information and check if you have what it takes to handle the kind of liabilities that their product entails. As such, poor financial management skills might affect your ability to secure a credit card for the business in the first place.

It also goes without saying that reporting your transactions to the reporting agencies can get mixed. For instance, you might get a credit report where your entries for both your personal and business transactions are made into your timeline. Of course, this means that any mark reported to that agency regarding your business credit card's transactions, whether good or bad, will affect your credit score.

4. Perks

Due to the fact that business cards are a bit more demanding to maintain, certain credit card issuers offer certain perks for those that do apply for such. The most common perks are discounts for payments of several utility services like electricity, Internet connection, and phone connection. Some issuers even provide discounts on Wi-Fi rates as well as office supplies which might be an advantage for businesses that rely a lot on these.

However, you might be more interested with flat-rate rewards programs where you can avail of certain bonuses every time you make a purchase with the card. It's best to consult with the issuer first before you submit your application so you know what rewards you can expect if you frequently use that card.

Personal vs. business: Which card should you choose?

As was stated, there is the option to use your personal credit card over a business credit card for most of your transactions. If you are still deciding whether to stick to your personal card or apply for a business card, there are certain factors that you should consider.

You might be better off with a business credit card if:

• You are a starting entrepreneur who wants to build your business's credit trustworthiness.

• You run a company whose expenses require a larger credit limit.

- Your expenses align most with reward categories that business cards offer.

- You no longer want to deal with low credit limits.

Who can apply for a business credit card?

Naturally, the first requirement you need to qualify for a business card is to have a business. So, if you don't have at least any form of business, does that mean that you are not qualified for a business credit card?

The answer, surprisingly, is no. You can actually qualify for a business credit card even if you are just interested in the rewards that these cards have.

The reason for this is quite simple: there is no strict definition as to what a "business" actually is. It could range from hawking wares at a flea market or running a corporation with a hundred employees in it. It doesn't even matter if your previous business experience involves setting up a lemonade stand outside your home.

So as long as the money you generated from your activities can be considered as business revenue, then you might find some use for a business credit card. Either way, the issuer will still look at your personal credit information to see if you have what it takes to meet the demands that the card entails.

However, a personal credit card might be for you if:

- You run a sole proprietorship whose business expenses fall below the usual personal credit card limits.

- Your expenses do not align with the rewards program most business credit cards offer.

- You are not interested in building credit for the business.

• You are not the one who would apply for a business loan anytime in the future.

Types of Business Cards

There are several business cards that you can apply for. They have the same functions and requirements but they will carry certain features that make them ideal in a number of situations. They are as follows:

1. Business Credit Cards

These are your typical credit card and they function mostly the same with a personal card. They have a credit limit that dictates how much you can use the card every month as well as how much you pay.

Whenever your card makes a charge, you are obligated to pay the charge each billing cycle. This doesn't mean you have to immediately pay the amount in full as you can pay in installments. Although, this does mean that you carry the balance month for month i.e. you will have to deal with interest rates until that debt is settled.

However, this does allow for a small financial cushion that small business owners can depend on during tough times.

2. Secure Business Cards

This card is ideal for businesses with little personal credit or none at all. Think of it as a credit builder card, only for business owners.

How it works is quite simple. When you apply for this card, you are required to deposit a minimum amount. This could be in between $2,000.00 and $5,000.00, depending on the card and the issuer.

This amount serves as your credit line and you can use that to pay for anything related to the business. Either way, every payment for that balance will be reported by the issuer to the credit reporting agency.

This way, your business can build up on its credit within a year. However, it's important to note that only on-time payments will be reported. Any payment you miss will be a derogatory mark, defeating the purpose of the card.

3. Business Charge Cards

Like the typical business card, charge cards have the same function as personal credit cards. However, they differ greatly in the aspect of credit limits since, basically, there is none.

Charge cards have something that is called as a "shadow" limit which tend to be higher than most credit card limits and can be flexible depending on the card holder's needs. They can also change depending on how often you use your card as well as the overall status of your credit history.

However, there is a catch: Going over the limit can cause your account to be frozen. Also, you can never carry your balance on a month to month basis. You'll have to pay the charge in full every billing period.

This card is recommended only for people who have full control over their spending habits. If you can spend only on what you can afford, this charge card might be ideal for you.

How to get a business credit card

The process of securing your business's credit card is surprisingly easy. In fact, the process is quite similar to getting a personal credit card. However, there are differences in the details that you will submit to the issuing company. Since this is a business credit card, then it would be apparent that the issuer would ask information regarding your business. The application form will include questions like:

- The legal name of the business

- Address

- The type of industry it belongs to. Some industries are considered high-risk and high-maintenance which could affect the approval of your application.

- The structure of the company whether you are a sole proprietorship, a partnership, or a corporation.

- The age of the business i.e. how long it has been operating.

- Number of people employed as well as the organizational structure.

- Annual revenue

- Estimated monthly expenditures and other finance-related matters.

It really depends on the institution as to what kind of information that they want from you. To make it easier on your part, it's best to look for the information on your part and prepare your documents and answers beforehand.

What you need to secure a quick approval

In the end, it is up to the discretion of the bank or any similar financial institution to decide whether or not to approve your application for a business credit card. To make them easily decide for your approval, there are a few things you have to do beforehand:

1. Have a Good to Excellent Personal Credit Score

Your personal credit score will actually influence how your application is going to be treated. That lender would have to make sure that you as the applicant have what it takes to meet the demands of the card.

For this, they would pull up a hard search on your personal credit history and look for any mark made regarding your financial activities. What one creditor would look for is different from another but it's safe to say that applicants with a history of on-time payments, good credit utilization rates, and minimal to no derogatory marks tend to have a better chance of getting their applications approved.

2. Have a Business

Although you don't exactly have to have a business to qualify for a business credit card, having one does tend to improve your odds of successfully securing one. The lending institution would most likely want to make sure that whatever credit or money you can secure through the card would be used to invest for an actual venture. One proof that you have a business is through securing an Employer's Identification Number from the Internal Revenue Service as well as opening a business account.

What transactions could the business credit card be used for?

There is actually no hard and fast rule as to where and how you should use your business's credit card. It has the same functions as your typical credit card albeit with a larger credit limit and a few more restrictions/obligations on your part.

The question, then, is not on where your business credit card will be the most applicable but on how to optimize its usage while minimizing the risks it entails. To do those, here are a few tips to keep in mind.

1. Set Limits

The 30% rule for personal credit card utilization rates apply here as well. If possible, do not go beyond 30% of the available credit when using the card. If the limit is at $10,000.00, then your spending should not be over $3,000.00.

Of course, there is a chance when the policy you have set up would not work in all situations. Some authorized users for the card might have different purposes in mind for it. This is where a bit of creativity comes into play.

You might set different limits for each user but you must set other limiters as well. For example, one user might only access the card for a certain set of situations or you rotate possession of the card to the different users on a bi-weekly basis. The point is to make sure that nobody gets to use the card for too long to avoid abuses.

2. Keep Everything Strictly Within Business

Even if you are running a sole proprietorship, resist any urge to use that card to spend for personal concerns. Keeping your business expenses separate from your personal one is one way to keep track of your expenses and claim deductions when taxing season comes around.

If you authorize your employees to use the card also, give guidelines as to what will qualify as a business expense. Having a system set up where employees have to seek approval before using the card and furnish receipts is a good way of enforcing accountability and limiting the card's use.

3. Make a Policy

If you are running a corporation, chances are your partners will also want to have access to that card. This would be an opportunity for you to draft a policy on how to use that card.

Make it a point to show to everyone that the card is accessible but only if they meet certain conditions and follow the guidelines. The point here is to be as transparent as possible in telling your staff and your partners who can use the card and for what purposes.

201

Chapter 14: Money And Position Management

The most standard system executed in trading is cutting adversities and riding productive positions to ensure that mishaps are inside reasonable cutoff focuses. This presence of mind procedure joins a position limit, a loss limit, and clear peril. A position limit is the most extraordinary proportion of any money a dealer allows to carry on, at any single time. Whereas, a loss limit is a measure planned to avoid unsustainable setbacks made by traders by means of techniques for setting to stop disaster levels. It is fundamental that you have stop-loss orders in place. In a clear system, intermediaries use guidelines when attempting to control change scale risk to measure their arranged increments against their possible mishaps. The thinking is that most traders will lose a double indistinguishable number of times from their profits, so a direct guideline for trading is to keep your danger/compensate extent to 1:3.

The idea of a stop loss is to help a trader have a small stop loss and avoid emotions from controlling the decisions you make.

The Risk/ Ration Reward

It is good to have a risk/reward ratio of 1:3 or 1:2. In other words, the trader is ready to risk $2 per share and make $4 per share — a risk/reward ratio of 1:1 means that you can't enter a trade because it is not worth that risk.

For experienced traders, they know where to set a stop loss. You won't find these traders wondering where to place a stop loss. Instead, they are much aware that once they open a trade position, they want the best risk/reward ratio.

When to set stop losses?

The best time for you to set up stop loss is the same time when you place an order. Don't start to wonder or guess. So once you place an order, you set your stop loss immediately because if you wait, you'll start to worry. Also, when feeling worried, you may end up placing it in the wrong place. That may cost you a lot.

Where to Set Stop Loss

There is no exact answer to this question, but there are some tips to follow when you want to set a stop loss in forex trading. Before you read the tips, here are some of the common mistakes that most traders make.

1. Placing a stop too tight

When you have a close stop loss, chances are that it will be stopped early. The forex market is volatile, and that means that you should not have a very tight stop loss. Traders afraid of losing their money place a close stop loss. As a result, they minimize the potential of losing their money. The trick with a tight stop loss is that you will have a lot of small losses that add up to form a significant loss.

2. Placing a wide stop loss

While a tight stop loss is bad, an extensive stop loss is discouraged. Some traders don't want their stop loss to be reached, and so they place a very wide stop loss. Although it is rare for an extensive stop loss to be activated, when it happens, the loss is even huge.

So what is the best thing to do? You have to go for something that is in between a vast stop loss and a tight stop loss. Take time to monitor the movement in price. When you don't see a trend, don't trade. When the trend is powerful, that should be easy for you to identify the sequence.

Placing a Stop Loss below the Last Low

You can still place a stop loss at the last significant low when you are in a long position. When the trend is stable, you should make some profit. But when the trend is weak, you'll be stopped out. That is okay because the price will go lower than the stop loss. The same applies in a downtrend. You could be looking forward to placing your stop loss above the last high.

Set Stop-Loss in a Downtrend

In case the downtrend goes past the previous high, then buyers should attempt to take over the control. You don't want to run short in this case, so you should close your position and look for other opportunities.

Increasing the Stop Loss

Many forex traders don't like to use this technique, yet it is the best. First, you place your stop loss once you open a trade. There are times when you'll get stopped fast, but the trade should continue. However, the most critical point comes when you have a profitable trade position. Can it change and shake your stop loss?

When faced with this situation, increase your stop loss to the entry point. That means if the price goes against your position, you won't lose a single dollar. That leads to another interesting question. When is the right time to increase the stop loss? Well, don't do it immediately when you make a profit. Wait for some time and monitor the trade. You need to master how to play around with your system but in a smart way.

Sometimes, the price may continue to rise when you expect it to drop. In this case, continue to increase your stop loss even further. By increasing your stop loss, you will be protecting your profit. When the price doesn't reach your target, close the trade with the profit that you have made. This is an example of trailing stop loss because the stop loss rises as the price increases. There are other methods that you can use to trail stop loss. That is for you to find out. Remember, it is from trying out that you find the best one to use.

The 1% Rule

Some traders use the 2% rule. The 1% rule requires traders to risk only 1% of their trading capital on any single trading position. However, because of small capital, many traders don't follow this rule. The best thing about this rule is that even when you have ten losing trades, you'll still retain a good percentage of your money. So you can see why you should train yourself to follow the 1% rule. Whether you have $100 in your account or more than $100, learn to use this rule if you don't want to lose all your money. Forex trading can be risky, especially when the market is volatile. Nobody will force you to use this rule, but you should make it a habit of using it in any trade that you open.

When trading with Fibonacci numbers, it is pretty easy to use stop losses. For example, if you want to join a long-term trading position, you must wait until when a correction happens to the retracement line. Stop loss is a critical topic. Each trader has their way of doing it. So you should also find yours. Create your trading plan and test out different ways of placing a stop loss. You will take time before you discover the best way suitable for you.

Money management tips

Is there a secret to success in forex trading? No. But there are a few things that all successful traders do, and are no secret. You merely have to be smart with money management.

Money management is not a new term in forex. It is just the knowledge and skill you use to manage your Forex trading account. That is the secret to a long successful trading career. Although many traders forget to use it, this section outlines ground rules that you can follow to control your account effectively.

Don't be carried away with making big money. This may cause you to lose a lot of money. There is no easy money in forex trading. To be successful in trading, you must learn to be patient and learn to trade small. Not all trades will give you profits. That is why you should plan on losses.

Another thing that you must do is to risk a small percent of your money on each trade. By doing this, you will reduce the risk of losing all your money. You can risk either 1% or 2% of your money. However, experienced traders go as high as 5%, but not more than that. Remember. It is easy to lose money in forex, but hard to regain.

Use Limit Orders

Successful traders know how to use a stop loss. Stop loss will control how much profit you make. A stop loss order will protect your investment and allow you to make small gains.

The Size of Your Trades

Traders are advised to open small trading positions. One of the reasons for this is because when you have a losing trade, you can decide to open another reverse trade position to compensate your losses.

Learn To Practice with Virtual Money

There is a good reason why the virtual method of trading was invented. Don't ignore it. Test all your trading strategies with virtual money before you start to trade on a real trading account. When you switch to actual trading, don't stop to use a virtual account when you want to test a new strategy. Don't risk your money on a real account that may cause you to lose all your money.

Tip

It is easy to master money management tips, but not easy to stick to it. But if you can discover the best money management methods that work for you, continue to use it and don't be carried away with the greed to make more money.

TRADING JOURNAL

One of the things that seasoned traders will tell you is that, more often than not, trading isn't about finding the secret "recipe" to success. It is mainly about having discipline. We have already seen why discipline plays a vital role in your trades. However, one of the ways that you can maintain discipline is by keeping a record journal. Institutional traders, regardless of their rank and their degree of success are trained to keep a journal until the habit of recording their transactions and other behaviors becomes automatic. The main reason for this was to instill a sense of accountability. After all, these traders are dealing with millions of dollars. How did these traders maintain their journal?

One of the habits that they formed was that for every long and short position that they made, for every stop-loss point they set up, every risk-reward ratio that they decided upon, they had to have a solid rationale for doing so.

It was always, "I am doing this because of the following reasons that are based on large amounts of research and information."

They never decided something without a strong foundation to carry their decisions.

Which is why this level of accountability leads to the formation of some of the best traders in the world. You might think that this is an extreme practice and only pertains to traders who are dealing with large sums of money.

On the contrary, it becomes even more important to you.

Why?

Because you are not dealing with someone else's money. You are using your own money.

For banking traders, they receive a fixed paycheck regardless of how poorly they perform. Of course, repeated mistakes mean that they are asked to leave the job. But in essence, they don't have any personal loss. In your case, forget getting a paycheck. If you lose, you are slowly drying up your own reserves. Additionally, institutional traders have multiple chances to make the money back without disrupting their personal lives. If you experience a loss, then you might find your entire life upended. Now, your journal is different from the checklist and questions that were created when you were building your trading plan.

Currency Pair Information

In this section, you are going to make notes about the currency pairs and how you have traded with them. This will work best if you have prepared a table and then taken a print out of the sheet.

Target Trades

In this section, you are going to list all the trades that you are going to make. Essentially, you are waiting for the current trade to generate its results so that you can proceed with your next trade.

Let's say that currently, the date is November 1.

Your entry should look something like this:

November 2

    Buy USD/CAD at 1.1712

    Stop loss placed at 1.1700

    Target 1: 1.1760

    On reaching Target 1, Target 2: 1.1790

    No Target 3. High Risk.

With just a few instructions, you have made your next task easier. You have given yourself clear instructions. The next day, let us assume that you had one of those mornings where you just can't seem to find the energy to even move your pinky.

You force yourself out of bed and realize that you need to get back to trading. However, you are in no mood to think straight. What do you do? How can you keep your trades going? Is this the end of the world? Wait! There is no need to panic. After all, you have already set a plan into motion. Everything will be okay!

Completed or Existing Trades

Of course, just like you have planned for future trades, you should also be recording your completed or existing trades. Spend some time looking through the trades you have already made to find out any mistakes you may have made. However, not only can you use this section to identify the losses, you might just discover a trend that you wouldn't have otherwise noticed while looking at the charts.

Think of it this way.

When you are talking with your friend, you might inject your responses and questions with a lot of "uhms" and "ahs". However, do you know how many of these blanks are inserted into one sentence? Are you aware of the frequency of these blanks? If you start recording your conversation and then play it back later, you might be surprised by the results.

Reporters and newscasters often record the way they speak and play it back to themselves so that they can improve their speech patterns. They can identify when they are most likely to pause and where they tend to lose track of the conversation.

In a similar way, you are using your journal to track the "uhms" and "ahs" of your trading. You might not be aware that you are making minor mistakes, but when you look through your journal, you might just be surprised by the frequency at which certain actions slip by your awareness.

RISK MANAGEMENT

The risk is that you'll lose money. But risk comes in many different forms and from many different sources. Sometimes the biggest risks are the ones that you never knew existed.

I believe forewarned is forearmed. In this section, I look at some of the main sources of risk that may not be readily apparent or that are easily overlooked.

Here are some basic risks that are associated with currency trading:

Exchange rate risk

Exchange rate risk is the cause of changes in the value of the currency. It relies upon the effect of relentless and largely precarious moves in the general free market action balance. For the period the representative's position is outstanding, the position is at risk to all esteem changes. This danger can be huge and depends on an accessible perspective of which way the financial models will move reliant on each possible factor that happens (or could happen) at some arbitrary time, anywhere on the planet.

The trading outside of the currency trade market is unregulated as it was before, esteem margin limits are not constrained as they were used traditionally for coordinated rate exchanges. The market moves subjected to key and concentrated components progressively.

Interest rate risk

Credit charge risk or interest rate risk suggests the advantage and adversity delivered by instabilities in the forward spreads, closed by forwarding total perplexes and maturity gaps among trades in the currency trade book. This danger is significant to money swaps, forward outright, destinies, and alternatives. To restrain financing cost risk, one should set confines on the hard and fast size of confounds. An ordinary strategy is to detach the mismatches, in perspective of their advancement dates, in up to a half-year and ongoing months. All of the trades are entered in automated systems in order to figure the circumstances for all of the dates of the movement, increments, and hardships. Steady examination of the advance cost condition is vital to check any movements that may influence on the exceptional openings.

Credit risk

Credit risk insinuates the probability that a remarkable money position is not to be repaid as agreed, in view of conscious or programmed action by a counter-party. Credit risk is usually something that is the stress of associations and banks. For the individual representative (trading margin), credit chance is very low as this, and it furthermore stays consistent for associations selected in and overseen by the specialists in European countries. Starting late, the National Prospects Association (NFA) has borne witness to their ward over the currency trade market promotions in the US and continue making a move against unregistered currency trade firms.

The known types of credit risk are as follows:

Substitution Risk

This occurs when counter-gatherings of a fizzled bank or currency trade agent discovers that they are in danger of not getting their assets from the fizzled bank.

Settlement Risk

This occurs in perspective of the diversification of time zones on different territories. In this manner, money related measures are traded at different expenses at different events in the midst of the trading day. Australian and New Zealand Dollars are credited first, then the Japanese Yen, trailed by the European money related measures and then fulfillment with the US Dollar. Thus, payment should be made to a party that will report liquidation or be broadcast obligated, before that party executing its own special portions.

In credit risk, the specialist must consider not simply the market estimation of their money portfolios, but also the potential introduction of these portfolios.

The potential presentation is to be determined by probability examination over the time to maturity of the phenomenal position. The electronic structures directly available are useful in realizing credit chance game plans. Credit lines are successfully checked. In addition, intermediaries for recognition of technique execution use the planning structures introduced in foreign exchange since April 1993. Intermediaries input the hard and fast credit augmentation for a specific counter-party. In the midst of the trading session, the credit expansion is thus adjusted. If the line is totally used, the system will keep the merchant from further dealing with that counter-party. After improvement, the credit line comes back to its one of a kind measurement.

Counter-party default risk

The danger that the principals with a trader, the intermediary's bank, or currency trade market, or the counter-parties with which the bank or currency market trades, will be not capable or will decrease to execute concerning such contracts.

In addition, principals in the spot and forward business divisions have no duty to continue making markets in the spot and forward contracts that are traded.

The budgetary dissatisfaction of counter-get-together could result in significant incidents. Yet again, while trading outside financial structures on an OTC introduce, the trader or customer will oversee associations as principals and establishments may be at risk to setbacks or liquidation. In case of any bankruptcy or mishap, the trader can recover, even in respect to property underlying under his or her record. For example only a certain amount of his traded currency will be handed over to the counter-party.

This particular section of a trader are handled by FCM (Futures Commission Merchant) to confirm that exchange-traded prospects will be subjected to the confined regulatory confirmations overseen by the client segregation rules and procedures.

Country and Liquidity Risk

The liquidity of OTC currency trade will be significantly more noticeable than that of exchange-traded cash in the future. However, the non-exchangeable scenario is seen, especially outside of US and European trading hours.

Additionally, a couple of nations or social occasions of nations have in the past constrained trading limits or repressions on the total expense on currency trading.

Remote exchange rates may vary in the midst of a given time period. The volume which may be traded using certain limitations for trading on positions is believed to produce absolute margin after some time.

Such cutoff focuses may shield trades from execution in the midst of a given trading period. Such impediments or cutoff focuses could keep a trader from a split-second trading in unfavorable positions and subsequently could uncover the specialist's record to liberal adversities.

Additionally, even in circumstances where Foreign Exchange costs have not ended up being subject to managerial restrictions, the General Assistant may be not capable to execute trades at great expenses if the liquidity of the market is not acceptable. It is also useful for a nation or social occasion of nations to constrain the trading of financial guidelines across over national edges. Suspend or bind the exchange or trading of particular money, issue very new fiscal principles to dislodge old ones, mastermind snappy reimbursement of particular cash duties, or demand that trading particular cash could be coordinated for liquidation in a manner of speaking. OTC currency is traded on different non-US markets, which may be liberally more slanted to times of non-liquidity than the Bound-together States promotes in view of a combination of components.

Besides, even where stop setback or limit orders are set up to undertake to compel incidents, these solicitations may not be executable in very frozen state exhibits or may be filled at unforeseeable repulsive esteem levels where non-liquidity or unprecedented shakiness keep them inexorably for great execution.

Marginal Risk

Low edge stocks or currency trade guarantees are typically required in currency trade, (similarly likewise with directed item prospects). These edge approaches allow a high level of use. As needs are, a moderately little value development in an agreement may result in prompt and generous misfortunes in an overabundance of the sum contributed. For instance, if at the season of procurement, 10% of the cost of an agreement were saved as edge, a 10% decline in the cost of the agreement would, on the off chance that the agreement was finished off, result in a complete loss of the edge store before any derivation for business commissions. A decline of over 10% would result in an all-out loss of the edge stock. A few merchants may choose to submit up to 100% of their record resources for edge or guarantee for foreign trade. Brokers ought to know that the forceful utilization of use will build misfortunes amid times of troublesome execution.

Transactional Danger

Errors in the correspondence when dealing with a merchant's demands may result in startling mishaps. Routinely, even where an out trade is liberally the fault of the overseeing counter-party establishment, the customer's arrangement of activity may be obliged in searching for compensation for coming about setbacks in the record.

Risk of Run

Indeed, even where a dealer/client's medium to long-term perspective of the market might be eventually right, the merchant will most likely be unable to monetarily shoulder momentary hidden misfortunes, and may finish off a situation at a misfortune basically in light of the fact that the individual can't meet an edge call or generally continue such positions. In this manner, even where a dealer's perspective of the market is right, and a cash position may at last pivot and wind up as productive, merchants with inadequate capital may encounter misfortunes.

216

Chapter 15: Goal Setting

After dealing with your debts and saving for an emergency fund, the next step is to plan what you will use your money for. Allocation of resources is one of the most basic problems that the study of economics tries to deal with. This problem exists because we have a limited amount of resources and an endless list of needs and wants.

The key to solving this problem on a personal level is to identify the needs and wants that you want to prioritize the most. You may do this by looking into the different options where you can spend your money on and identify the ones that you really want to work for.

How to Plan and Set Your Stock Trading Goals

Let's start with the first step:

Step 1: Identifying Future Goals and Expenses

Setting a solid financial goal starts with your ideas. You may start by thinking of the things that you want to buy in the future. Most of us are already doing this. However, only a few actually do more than think about their dreams. Instead, most people only do wishful thinking and hope that one day they will have enough money to achieve their goals.

To start your own goal setting process, make a list of the things that you want to buy in the future. Some of the things that you may have in your list may be really important like buying a home or setting up a retirement fund. Others, like taking a big vacation or buying a sports car are not as important but they may make us happier.

After creating your list, put a number beside each item with the number 1 assigned to the most important goal. Here is a sample list that you can base your own on:

1. Create a Wedding Fund

2. Buy a home that's big enough for the family

3. Save for kids' college fund

4.   Save for dream travel destination

Some goals have a predetermined deadline. If you have kids for example and you are saving for their college fund, the fund needs to be ready by the time they graduate from high school.

Step 2: Setting a Target Amount

When working for your financial goals, you need to deal with them one at a time. While we want to achieve all the goals in our list, we are more likely to accomplish goals faster when we focus our financial resources on the ones that are most important to us. When that particular goal is done, we could move on the next task on our list.

Step 3: Planning the Saving Timeline

Now that you have your financial goals set, pick the most important one and set the timeline for saving for that goal. By plotting the timeline, you will be able to know how long you have to save for the goal.

As we've discussed in the previous chapter, it's best to invest in the stock market only for your long term goals to lessen the risk. Pick a financial goal that is still a couple of years away from completion and set it as the target of your stock investing activities.

Step 4: Assess the amount of growth you need to reach your goals

The general idea behind investing is that you will need to make your savings grow so that you will reach your financial goals faster. You want to set the right expectations when it comes to the growth potential of your investments. Some of your trades will yield north of 15% while others will end up with losses. It is more realistic to expect a modest rate of return of 7% to 10% each year. Some beginners who make early mistakes in the stock market may experience even lower rates of return on their first few years of trading. While these rates of return may seem low, they are still better than many of the investment opportunities out there.

Knowing the average rate of return in the market, you will be able to make assumption on how long it will take for your funds to grow to reach your target amount. If you have $10,000 right now and you invest it and get an average of 8% rate of return per year, it will take you more than 9 years to reach a $20,000 target. You can increase the rate of reaching that target by adding more capital to your fund each month. You may also increase the rate of growth by taking high growth rate stocks in the beginning of the trading period.

To learn the relationship of the rate of return to the amount of time it takes you to reach your goal, use a compounding interest calculator. In this type of calculator, you will need to enter the capital amount, the number of years that you will be investing, and the annual rate of return you are expecting to get the final amount. Any additional income you earn in the market will be reinvested to it to create a compounding effect. This will help you reach your target amount faster.

Step 5: Practice with Paper Trading

If you find that the stock market is the best place to invest for your financial goals, you can increase your chances of success by practicing your trades. You can start practicing by doing trades on paper.

You can start a paper trade by taking a notebook and taking notes of the stocks that you want to invest in. You could then start by choosing one of these stocks and do a mock trade. In your mock trade, you pick the stock; you also identify your buying price and the volume of your purchase. Lastly, you set the conditions where in you will sell the stock. In the following days, months or years, you could then start to track the stock that you picked to assess the performance of your mock trade.

You could make the mock trade even more realistic by creating a budget that is similar to the budget that you will have when you actually start trading. This will prevent you from being reckless in your stock picks.

Mock trades like this allow you to practice with your trading strategies. If your mock trades often end up with losses, you may need to make changes in your trading strategy.

Paper trades also allow you to become more familiar with the market and the different events that are going on in the moment before you even participate in the market. It allows you to experience how it would be like to invest in the companies that you consider to be within your circle of competence.

The key to paper trading is to do it as many times as you can. This will allow you to know which indices, sectors and companies are most profitable.

Step 6: Get Started

Now that you know what you want to achieve and what you need to achieve it, start working on your financial goals. You can begin by saving for your investment capital. Ask your broker for the minimum amount that you will need to start investing. While you are saving, start studying the companies that you will buy with your initial investment amount. This will ensure that you will be ready to start investing when you have saved the minimum investing amount needed.

How Many Trades Per Month?

The costs incurred by those who enter into a mutual fund are the following:

- The entry or subscription commission paid at the time of the first payment.

- The management fee, on the other hand, is the cost borne by the cross-party fund manager. It is calculated on an annual basis, but generally paid on a six-monthly, quarterly or monthly basis.

- The extra-commission of performance is instead an optional commission that some self-financing funds in order to reward if, thanks to their ability, the fund's return exceeds a certain threshold based on pre-established parameters

How Much Money is it Going to Take?

As time goes by, you can see that there are other funds you can invest in and hold for a decade or so. If you can locate the right fund, you should do that. When a decade ends, you will be the successful owner of two or probably three funds, but you should not over-diversify your funds. You see, there is no reason for that. You can spread your money among an aggressive growth fund, a value-type growth fund, a global fund, and a small cap fund. **A tip:** If you have bought a growth fund that invests in more aggressive stocks, it should go up several folds in a bull market scenario and have a spectacular fall, as compared to the general market during bearish years. The key to survive it is not to panic, but instead keep your eye on the years ahead when you will be able to make millions from these very funds.

Risk Management

With the help of safe investing, there are some of the rules which you have to learn to have the investment safe and not spend all the money which you have hard earned with letting it go to waste. It is the fear which does not make most of the people invest in stocks because where there is profit; there is a risk as well. You may be lucky to get the instant benefit out of it, but you have to know these rules to be on the safe side.

Safe Types of Investment

You have to check over the type of investment which is working out best for you. There are five different types which are reliable such as the money market account, treasury, CDs, bank savings, securities, and the fixed annuities. With keeping the consideration understood, you have to make safe investments for yourself. You have to figure out the way to make sure that your primary purpose is to protect yourself and have the right side over these priorities becoming your strength. There are some high ends, and on the other hand, there will be losses which can be depressing to see the best interest for yourself.

Learn about investments

There are no safe investments, so you have to see which the safest one for you are. You have to learn about the risks which are associated with it to know which one is the safest option for you according to your situation. As there is no one law for you to learn about it, you have to check out the one which is ideal for you. There are many losses which the people may face along with handling the information which is not liable for them.

With the help of liquidating assets, you pay a massive return to the economy making sure the there is enough money which is on the safe place. It helps in inflation and brings the economy to the right place as well. You have to make sure that there is nothing left with the system so that your amounts are safe and sound at the right time. There are some principals which you have to follow to keep the purchasing power at the end of the accounts with the stock market.

Figuring out the amount

It is entirely on you how you determine which amount you have to keep and which you have to invest. You have to build the safe side and no one will be taking that decision for you. As the funds start to come up, then you can think of the growth, but eventually, you have to make the decisions which are worthwhile and see the results on how it proceeds further.

Along with keeping the determination of withdrawing the money, you can spend the time in learning through the processes which are the true projection of the needs required for the cash flows. There are some of the safe investments which you can depend on and be on the other side of the accounts to have the withdrawal for your fund which are available in the right timings.

Realistic Rate

When you have the returns in place, there are investments which are through the income and how you have to invest through the safe accounts. It depends how long you take to invest in it but if you are a part of it then there is nothing to keep in the mind which can be beneficial on both of the aspects which are keeping the investments away.

If you own stocks, stocks or mutual price range, you're answerable for paying taxes for them. The charges will now not be simply paid on the time of promoting the stock, but the fees also are applicable for the earning you benefit from them if the capital profits are going definitely so as your income, you are much more likely to pay extra taxes on it.

There are some situations wherein the taxes are deductible. And you've a right to claim these taxes. The maximum not unusual way to pay the price is the expenses paid from the investors to the agents.

By means of promoting the stocks after finishing 12 months will reduce the tax liabilities. Hiring a professional accountant or economic adviser is essential for an investor. In any other case, you may reduce to rubble all of the financing due to the fact these approaches are so complicated and cannot be handled alone. Now if you are going to make investments within the stock marketplace or have already got invested, you realize what to do. In case you overlook some factors, let's take into account it quickly.

Considerations for Safe Investment

You can additionally avoid the taxes by buying the stocks in a tax-deferred account. You are not chargeable for paying the taxes handiest at the time of promoting the stocks; you'll be answerable for paying the taxes in your dividends. Here are such a lot of options accessible, presenting a ramification of different pricing programs.

If there may be a virtual tour, even higher! Possibilities are you'll be making all of your trades electronically and now not actual man or woman, so ensure you're relaxed with that (maximum brokerages fee better buying and selling costs for a real individual thru their smartphone line to area orders). You should spend almost as a variety of time learning agents as getting to know the real stocks you will purchase. Ensure to observe numerous assessment websites that look at the accessible alternatives and discover the only that excellent fits your making a funding wishes/desires. With the recent virtual improvements on Wall Avenue, possibilities are you'll be the usage of a web supplier. The internet web page will possibly even provide a studies platform to get actual-time quote and in-depth facts on organizations. This will help you in studying your businesses and make better funding alternatives.

Chapter 16: Nine Steps to Credit Repair

Repairing your credit takes nine steps, each of which will be discussed in greater detail in the next few pages.

1. Obtain a copy of your credit report from the three major credit bureaus (Experian, Trans Union Corp., and Equifax).

2. Highlight all negative items.

3. Challenge each of the negative items.

4. Request an updated credit report; check to ensure that some of the negative items were removed.

5. Repeat steps 2-4 once every two months until no additional items are removed.

6. Prepare a consumer statement disputing each of the remaining negative items, and request that the Credit Bureau include the statement in your credit file.

7. Request that each Credit Bureau furnish you with the names and addresses of each creditor still reporting a negative entry for your account.

8. Contact each of these creditors and attempt to negotiate a settlement.

9. Request that updated copies of your credit report be sent to anybody who received your credit report in the past six months.

These steps are all based on the rights granted to consumers through the Fair Credit Reporting Act (FRCA). As you implement the steps outlined above do note that the FCRA will not protect any request, challenge, or consumer statement that can be proven to be frivolous in nature.

It is highly unlikely that this charge will be made by a creditor or credit bureau, as they know that your defense can be that you were simply acting according to your understanding of your rights as granted by the FCRA.

Step One: Get a Copy of Your Credit Report

Before you can start to fix your credit report, you must first figure out what it contains. If you still have your credit reports that I suggested you get at the beginning of this book, go to step 2. If you don't have a copy of your report, then do the following:

Contact the three major credit bureaus, Experian Inc., Trans Union Corp., and Equifax Inc., to see which agency has a file on you. You might also want to contact other local credit bureaus, because there may be several different versions of your credit report floating around. It is a good idea to start with the three major credit bureaus and deal with others later.

Although you may save $8.00, in your effort to repair your credit, you don't need any unnecessary credit denials added to your credit report at this time. This is the exact kind of information that you are trying to erase from your file. However, if you don't have the $24.00 necessary to buy all three copies of your credit reports, this is an option.

There are other ways of learning about your credit report. Instead of the letter request, you can call the Credit Bureau and make an appointment to review your credit file in person. It is advisable that you wait for the Credit Bureau to tell you everything they know about your credit history before you volunteer any potentially damaging information to other parties.

Step Two: Note All Negative Items on the Report

Each Credit Bureau has their own way of organizing their credit reports. Make sure that you read and understand all the information they send on how to read their report. It is up to you to determine which entries are damaging.

Such items may include a different social security number, incorrect name or spelling of your name, wrong addresses, and excessive number of inquiries, charge offs, late payments, judgments, or anything else that will keep you from being granted new credit.

Perhaps your record was confused with another customer who has a similar name or social security number. Maybe the negative information is outdated, beyond the seven year legal reporting limit imposed by the FCRA.

Step Three: Challenge Each of the Negative Items

Send letters to each Credit Bureau, challenging each of the negative items on your report, even though they may be true.The Fair Credit Reporting Act (FRCA) states that any credit item that is challenged by a consumer must be proven by the creditor in order to be considered verified.

If this re-verification is not completed in a timely manner (approximately 30 days) or if the challenge goes unanswered, the affected negative credit items must be completely deleted from your file, never to reappear.

Note: Do not challenge more than four items at a time. Challenging more than four may cause the Credit Bureau to deem your challenge frivolous and deny your challenge.

Your challenges can be based on the argument that:

You never made late payments to that account

The account is not yours

You don't remember the facts as stated on your credit report

You don't remember applying for the credit card

There may be other arguments applicable to your particular situation. The challenging process works very well because there are many factors working to your benefit:

Certain negative items cannot be proven because they were legitimately in error and should have never been reported in the first place

Credit denials are often thrown out by creditors soon after they are received. As such, these items are generally not reconfirmed. Also, if the item is over two years old, there is a good chance that these records are not retained by the creditor.

If you have already paid off the account, the creditor will probably not want to be bothered and will not respond to the challenge.

A creditor might not respond within the time constraints set by the credit bureau in accordance with the FCRA's guidelines, generally about 30 days.

There is also the element of human error that can come into play (i.e. they may lose the challenge report, can't find the proof, things get lost in the mail, etc.) and result in a non-response by the creditor. The end result: the items are removed from your report. So, the odds are in your favor.

Step Four: Receive an Updated Credit Report

Within one month of challenging any negative items, you should receive an updated copy of your credit report (hopefully without some of the old negative items). If you have not received your new report within 6 weeks, call the credit bureau and remind them that you are waiting for the new copy of your credit report.

Step Five: Repeat this Procedure Once Every Two Months

Keep repeating steps 2 through 4 every two months until no additional items are removed as a result of your challenges. If the remaining creditors are determined to reconfirm their claims and continue to do so over and over again, it is time to move on to the next step.

Step Six: Prepare a Consumer Statement

Prepare a 100-word statement of dispute for each of the remaining negative items, and have the Credit Bureau include these statements in your credit file. These statements will show that the situation is still in dispute, and that there is another side to the story. You won't be declared unworthy of credit based on these claims, because they are still pending.

Step Seven: Request the Names and Addresses of Each Creditor

Explain to the Credit Bureau that there are still many mistakes on your credit report and that you would like to contact the creditors in question directly. Request that the Bureau send you the names, addresses, and phone numbers of each creditor still reporting a negative entry for your account.

Step Eight: Contact Each Creditor and Negotiate a Settlement

Negotiations between each creditor may differ depending on the circumstances. Creditors of unsecured loans are motivated to settle because after a certain amount of time these accounts are written off as a total loss; any payments would be considered to be "found" money, so you will probably have a very willing negotiating partner.

Step Nine: Ask That They Send Out Your Updated Credit Report

When your credit report is as clean as it's going to get, contact each Credit Bureau one more time. Request that updated copies of your credit report, be sent to all the creditors who received a copy of your credit report within the past six months.

Chapter 17: Appraise Your Current Financial Status

Now since you have decided to learn to manage your personal finances, let us start by appraising your current financial status. There are few questions you must ask yourself to know the equilibrium of your income and expenditure. Answer the following questions –

- Do you often encounter paucity of money for your daily expenses?
- Do you eat frequently out, thus spending a lot of money?
- Do you live paycheck to paycheck?
- Are you at the loss of words when asked how much is your household/personal expenses?
- Do you despise or dread sudden domestic expenditure?
- Have you ever planned your monthly budget?
- Do you save money for a longer or shorter perspective?

If there are more than 4 No as the answer to this questionnaire, your income and expenditure are not balanced and need immediate attention.

Scrutinizing Income vs. Expenses

It is vital to monitor our income and expenses and keep them in tandem. Any disparity in maintaining their equilibrium will result either in debts that would only be mounting and multiplying gradually. Spendthrift people often spend rashly and later on suffer financial setbacks that are often irreparable. Moreover, strict monitoring and streamlining of income and expenditure is going to render long-term benefits that would be felt in later stages of life.

Here are some genuine and practical tips to monitor our incomes and expenditures thus to make the most of our monetary funds -

Watch where you are Spending

It is a good money managing strategy to know your expenses to the maximum extent. There may be some unforeseen expenses that may rock your budget, but enough scope should be there in your monthly budget to accommodate them. Include all sorts of expenditures you come across in your day to day life starting from your groceries to your evening drinks. When the entire list of expenditure is going to be on paper, you will realize how much money is spent uselessly on frivolous things.

Cut down the Unnecessary Spending

Now once you have complete and comprehensive list of expenses with you, you know where you income would be going. Trust me; you will have an impulsive feeling to cut short many worthless expenses that may deem to you simply useless. And this very is the objective of listing all your expenses. You can also bifurcate them into categories like – important, less important and least important, etc. The idea is to sift the expenses that you can do without.

Do Not Overindulge

If you have good and steady income, it doesn't mean that all has to be spent and splurged. Spare money is to be saved and sorted so they can be used when the need may arise. For example, if the income is 2000 USD, do not make a budget of that whole amount. Save some money aside and do not count that for the purpose of spending.

Spend Wisely

Wise spending can't be learned or implemented in a single day. It is not a procedure, rather a habit that has to be developed over the time. One can't be a wise spender one particular month and then start splurging the next. Get into a habit of watching your money and then think practical while spending. Wise money management does not lay stress on being a miser or a money-stasher. It teaches how to be a smart spender so that the worth of every penny is derived out. Start in a small way – like cutting the bills of fast food snacks that tend to be heavy on health, as well as pocket. Instead of this, buy lots of fruits and keep them stocked at home. This will benefit your reckless spending as well as your health.

Escalate your income

Smart spenders and savers are always on the lookout of the chances and avenues that would help them in multiplying their income. If you are a school teacher, start taking tuitions in free time. If you are a chef, start taking cooking classes during the weekend. The idea is to augment the inflow of money via multiple streams. A small effort from your side will open many avenues for bettering your income.

Carry Debit/credit card instead of cash

Do not carry the lot of cash in your pocket else you would be spending the lot of it. Though there are people, who tend to spend more when they have their debit or credit cards in their pockets. Just follow a viable routine that would prevent you from spending recklessly.

Ways to Monitor Your Expenses

There are plenty of ideas, tools and applications that can be used for keeping a track of our incomes and expenditures. You just need to have the intention of using these, and they would take care of the rest of the things. Some of them are -

- **Mobile Phone App** – The latest smart phones come with one or the other kinds of applications that help in keeping the record of monthly income and expenditures.

- **Money Box** – Keep a money box handy in your home and use it to store all the receipts and bill that you pay. This will keep clarity of all expenditures. Also, keep in the box a piece of paper that has the record of income.

  - **Calculator** – There are specific budgetary calculators that help in maintain the record of expense

- **Diary/Note-book** - Maintain a small pocket diary or a notebook in which you can jot whatever you spend. You would know exactly what have you spent on daily, weekly, fortnightly or monthly basis.

Get Rid of Bad Debt

Debts are the most irksome factor that disturbs management of our personal finances. However, debts are not always bad. Interestingly, some of them are good also. The present economic scenario is making it sensible to pay for some of our purchases on credit so that one can make maximum use of their liquid cash. The credit taken will keep the factor of depreciation of money well in control with the help of the rate of interest.

The good debt must never be considered as a liability. It is rather an investment that tends to make our money grow over a longer period, giving us the chance to make optimal use of liquid cash. One apt example of good debt is education loan that is taken to pay for college or higher education. Taking an education loan doesn't always mean that the borrower cannot afford paying the fee in cash. This loan is also taken in order to take advantage of low-interest rate of education loan. Students avoid using the cash of their parents and start repaying their education loan soon after they complete their education and are ready to earn lucrative salaries. A mortgage is also considered to be a good debt as it is considered to be the money saver in the longer run. One can take help of mortgages for buying homes. This kind of debt comes with measly monthly payments while the liquid cash in hand can be used for some other purpose. Good debt is considered to be good for the fact that they come accompanied with the low rate of interest.

In contrast to good debts, bad debts are taken to buy those things or services that lose their worth fast and do not create any promising income in the long term. They also come accompanied with the higher rate of interest. One common example of bad debt is credit card debt that is known for creating a vicious circle of financial liabilities. Buying flashy and branded luxuries through your credit card and then feeling helpless over its non-payment for years to come is a classic example of bad debt. Other types of bad debts are cash advance loan and payday loan that charge astronomical rate of interests that get compounded if not paid on time. These kinds of loans are devised to take advantage of borrower's pathetic and helpless financial condition.

Don't allow accumulation of Bad Debt

Just like a debt can't be accumulated in a single day, it can't be resolved in on a distinct date. The primary requisite to manage our personal finances is to keep away from debts. If you already have few of them to irk you, start planning strategically.

Read below-listed suggestions that would make you wiser and judicious in developing money-saving habits –

Shun debt accumulation

If you are already debt-ridden, just stop there. Do not add more to your already loaded financial burdens. You ought to concentrate over resolving past financial liabilities, thus keep your further track clean and clear. There is no point in clearing one debt by taking two more. This way, your financial status is going to become murkier.

Don't Rely on Credit cards

Credit cards are the biggest reason and cause of bad debts. This financial product gives ready cash to spenders and makes them reckless and mindless spenders. Just keep them away and learn to live without them. Using a credit card simply makes for uncontrolled spending that leads to the further financial mess. Never close the credit card accounts until all debts against it are repaid back lest the credit score will get affected.

Develop sensible attitude

Debt accumulation does not happen out of need but out of lax attitude towards money. This calls for immediate change in attitude so that what causes debt can be cured. A strong will to develop a frugal and a judicious attitude towards money will certainly take care of many financial issues that are known to be caused due to irresponsible mind-set towards.

Alter your spending tendencies

Are you a mindless spender who buys not out of need but out of greed? If you are one such person who cannot restrain buying things that are not even needed, you need to cure yourself. Do not remain lounged in front of TV watching advertisements and ordering things online. Watching online shopping sites just as a hobby is a sure shot recipe for landing in debts. Buying just to look 'cool' in your friend circle will be financially suicidal.

Don't Allow Consumerism to overshadow your lifestyle

Since we live in the times of consumerism, we have started believing that there are many things that are simply indispensable for our subsistence. This is a wrong approach as we are the ones who are responsible for expanding our wants….mistaking them for needs. To ourselves debt-free we must trim our lifestyle and live in a thrifty way.

Add volume to your income

While cost cutting is always suggested for getting rid of debts, opening, multiple income channels will speed up the process. Better the income, more rapidly you would be able to shrug off your financial responsibilities. And moreover, earning extra is never going to hurt you in anyway. Income can be increased by doing any such thing that interests you. It could be either some money-making hobby of yours (like teaching cooking, music, dance or aerobics) or some skill (being a singer, writer or carpenter, etc.). Having an alternative income channel will cushion your financial crises.

Make timely payments for avoiding penalties

Understand that you are already in debt and paying extra and superfluous charges (that can be certainly avoided) will sap up your resources. Do not delay paying bills, do not jump traffic rules, do not drive while drunk as these are some of the cases where a lot of money get drained due to sheer negligence and carelessness. Some other ways to save precious money are –

- Withdrawing money from bank instead ATM

- Avoiding online booking of tickets

- Buying credit card after negotiating rate of interest

- Consolidating multiple loans into one single loan that has lower rate of interest

Making Budget and Abiding by It

Having a budget for your income and expenditure will help in streamlining your finances that are already ailing due to debts. Categorize your expenses and tweak them to fulfill all liabilities as and when required. You will start having a fair idea where and how much to spend, giving you complete control over your money matters.